ULTIMATE
Classic Rock
GUITAR COLLECTION

Project Manager: Aaron Stang
Art Layout/Design: Ken Rehm

ARTIST INDEX

CONTENTS

AMERICAN PIE

Words and Music by
DON McLEAN

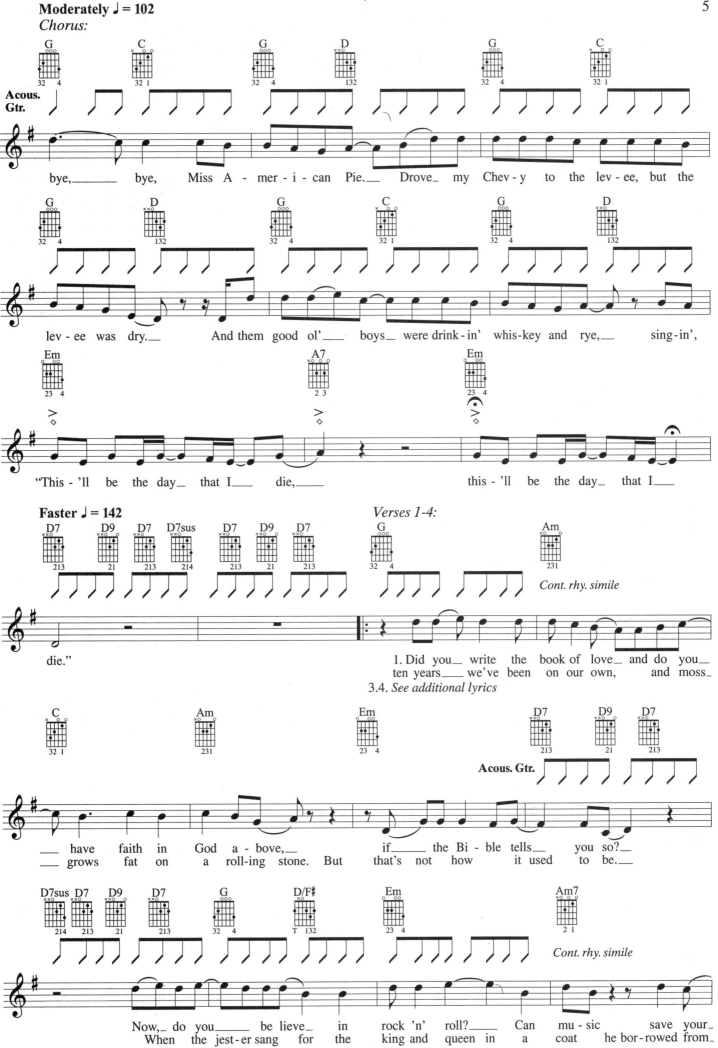

6

American Pie - 6 - 3

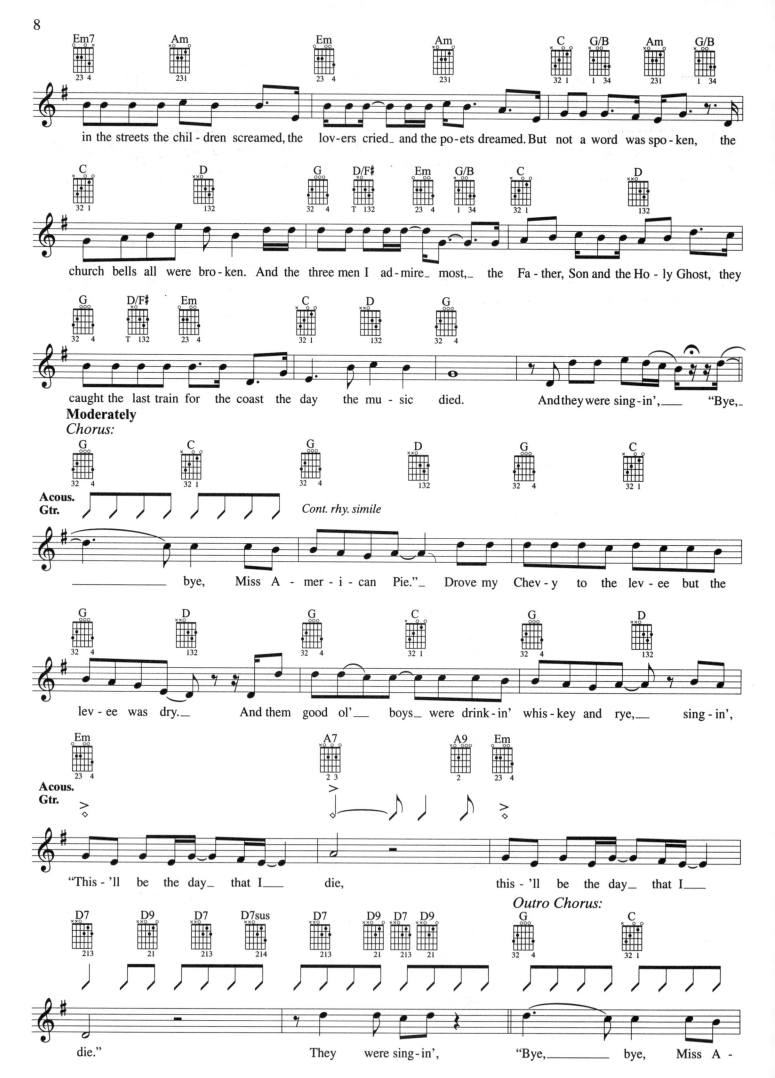

mer - i - can Pie."_ Drove my Chev-y to the lev-ee but the lev-ee was dry.__ Them

good ol'___ boys___ were drink-in' whis-key and rye,___ sing-in',

Acous. Gtr.

"This - 'll be the day___ that I___ die."___

Verse 3:
Helter skelter in a summer swelter,
The birds flew off with the fallout shelter,
Eight miles high and falling fast.
It landed foul on the grass.
The players tried for a forward pass
With the jester on the sidelines in a cast.
Now the halftime air was sweet perfume
While sergeants played a marching tune.
We all got up to dance.
Oh, but we never got the chance.
'Cause the players tried to take the field,
The marching band refused to yield.
Do you recall what was revealed,
The day the music died?
We started singin'...
(To Chorus:)

Verse 4:
And there we were all in one place;
A generation lost in space
With no time left to start again.
So come on, Jack be nimble, Jack be quick,
Jack Flash sat on a candlestick
'Cause fire is the devil's only friend.
And as I watched him on the stage,
My hands were clenched in fists of rage.
No angel born in hell
Could break that Satan's spell.
And as the flames climbed high into the night
To light the sacrificial rite,
I saw Satan laughing with delight,
The day the music died.
He was singin'...
(To Chorus:)

AQUALUNG

Words and Music by
IAN ANDERSON and JENNIE ANDERSON

12

Aqualung - 8 - 3

15

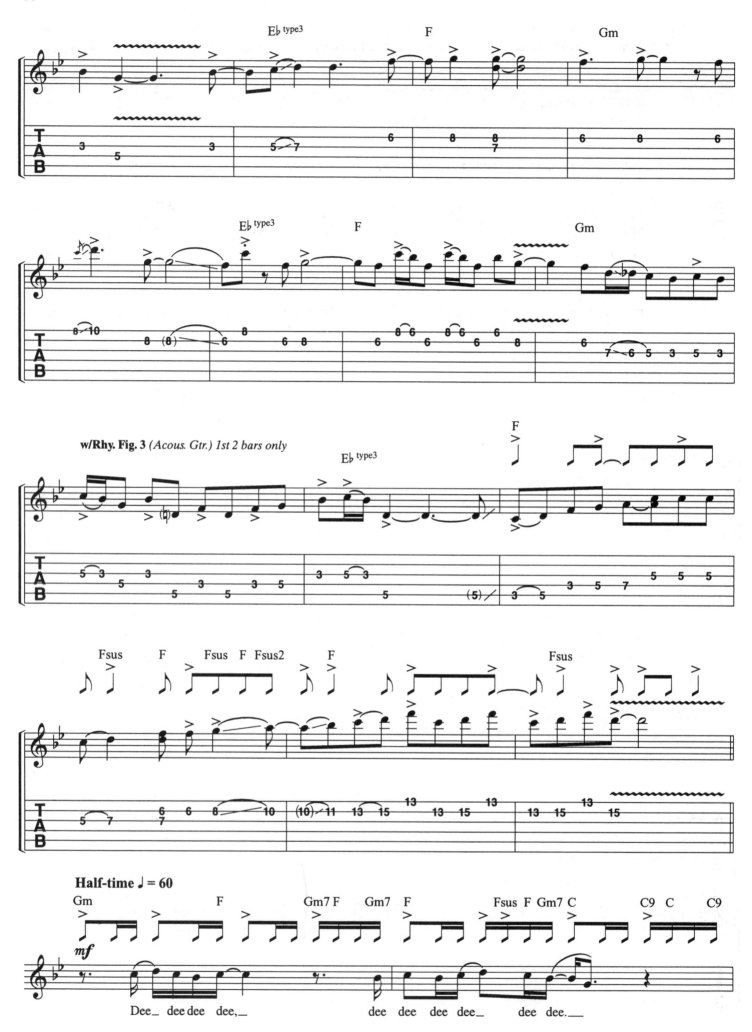

BORN TO BE WILD

Words and Music by
MARS BONFIRE

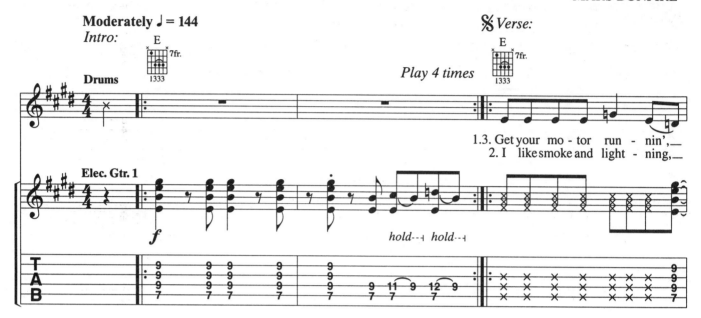

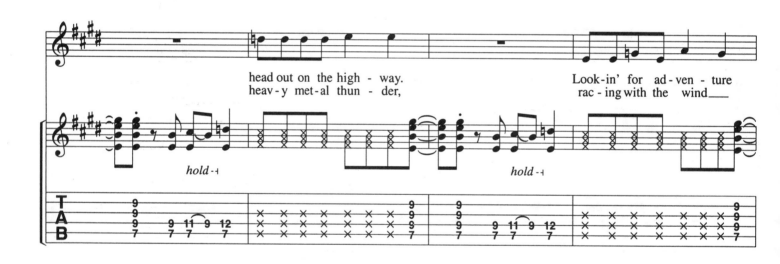

THE BOYS ARE BACK IN TOWN

Words and Music by
PHILIP PARRIS LYNOTT

The Boys Are Back in Town - 9 - 2

The Boys Are Back in Town - 9 - 4

Bridge

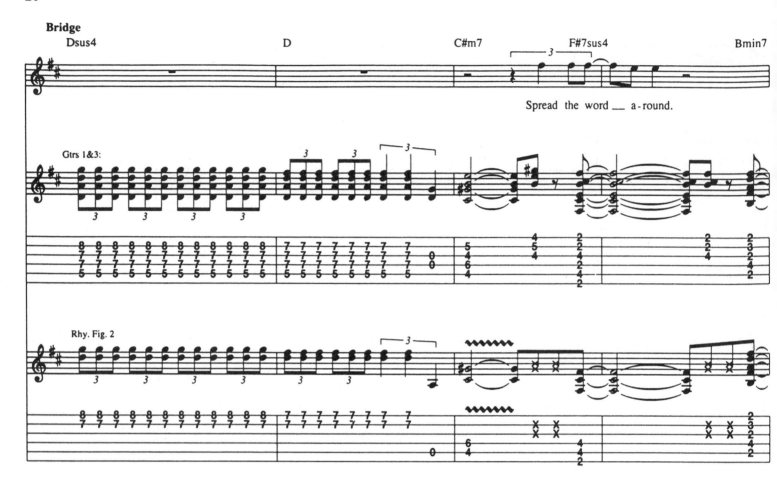

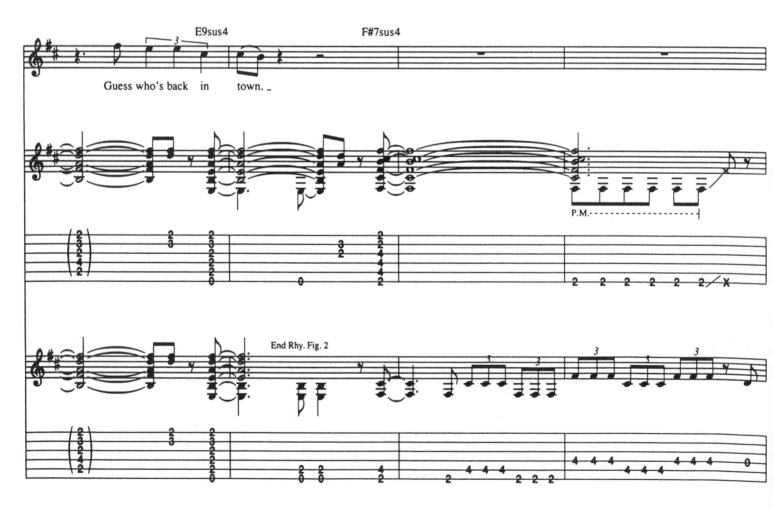

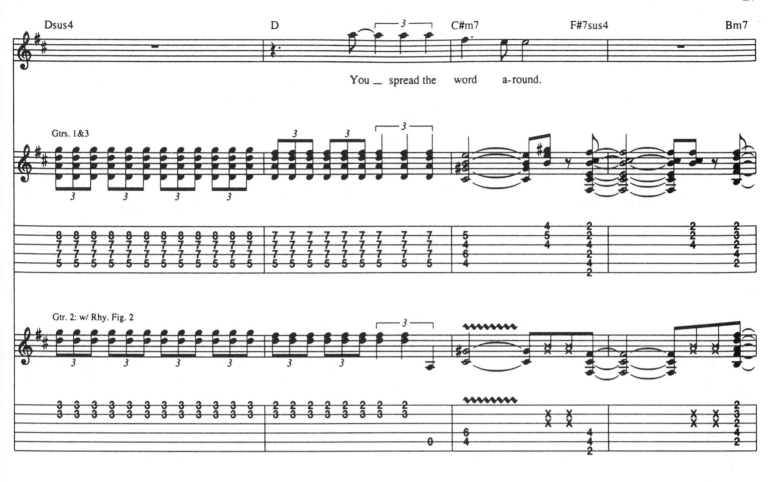

You __ spread the word a-round.

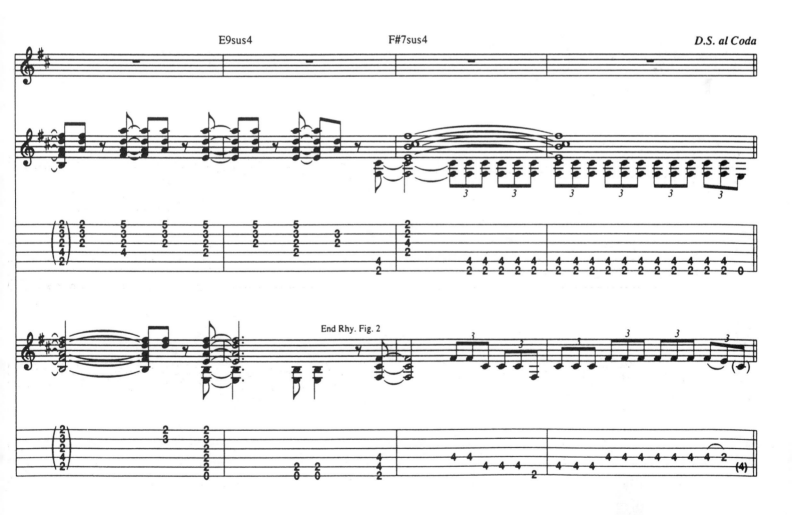

The Boys Are Back in Town - 9 - 6

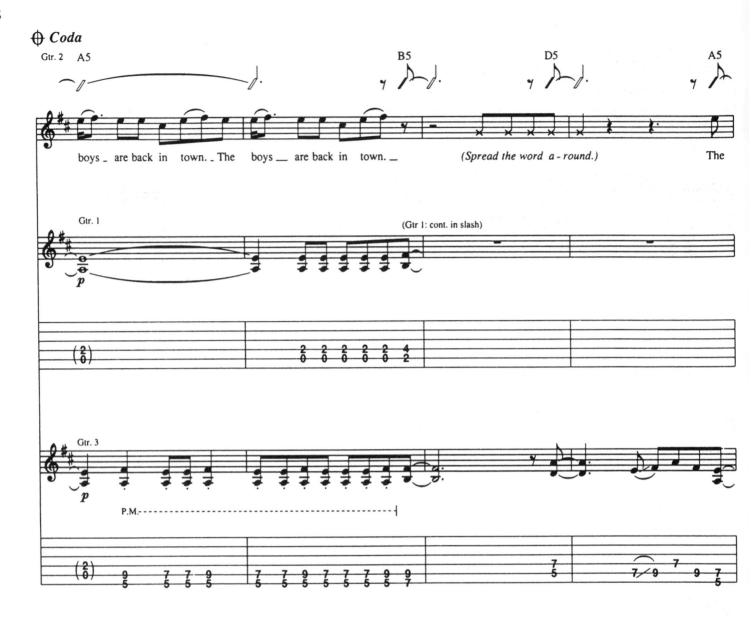

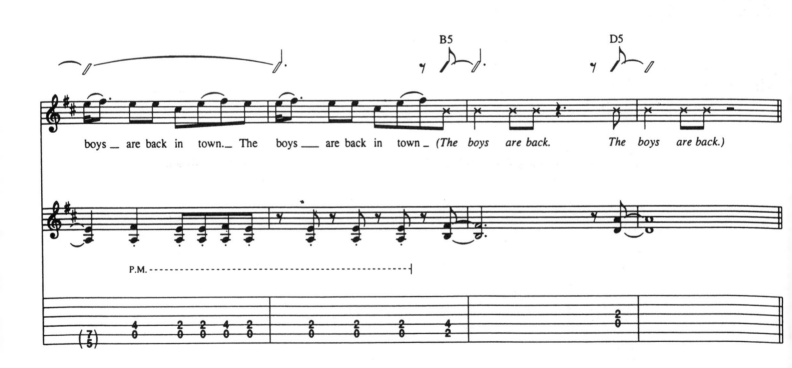

30

The Boys Are Back in Town - 9 - 9

CASEY JONES

Words by
ROBERT HUNTER

Music by
JERRY GARCIA

32

Casey Jones - 5 - 2

Verse 2:
Trouble ahead the lady in red,
Take my advise you'd be better off dead.
Switchman's sleeping train hundred and two is
On the wrong track and headed for you.
(To Chorus:)

Verse 4:
Trouble with you is the trouble with me;
Got two good eyes, but we still don't see.
Come 'round the bend, you know it's the end.
The fireman screams and the engine just gleams.
(To Chorus:)

Casey Jones - 5 - 5

CALIFORNIA DREAMIN'

Words and Music by
JOHN PHILLIPS and MICHELLE PHILLIPS

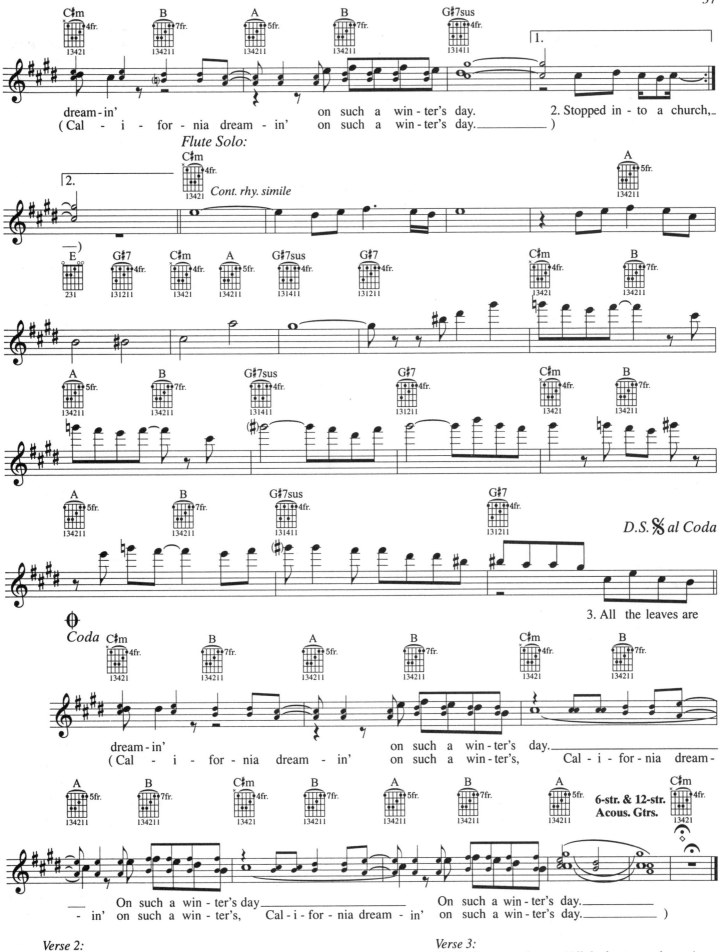

Verse 2:
Stopped into a church
I passed along the way.
Well, I got down on my knees (Got down on my knees.)
And I pretend to pray. (I pretend to pray.)
You know the preacher liked the cold (Preacher liked the cold.)
He knows I'm gonna stay. (Knows I'm gonna stay.)
(To Chorus:)

Verse 3:
All the leaves are brown (All the leaves are brown)
And the sky is gray. (And the sky is gray.)
I've been for a walk (I've been for a walk)
On a winter's day. (On a winter's day.)
If I didn't tell her, (If I didn't tell her,)
I could leave today. (I could leave today.)
(To Chorus:)

California Dreamin' - 2 - 2

CHANGES

Words and Music by
DAVID BOWIE

*Chords derived from overall tonality.

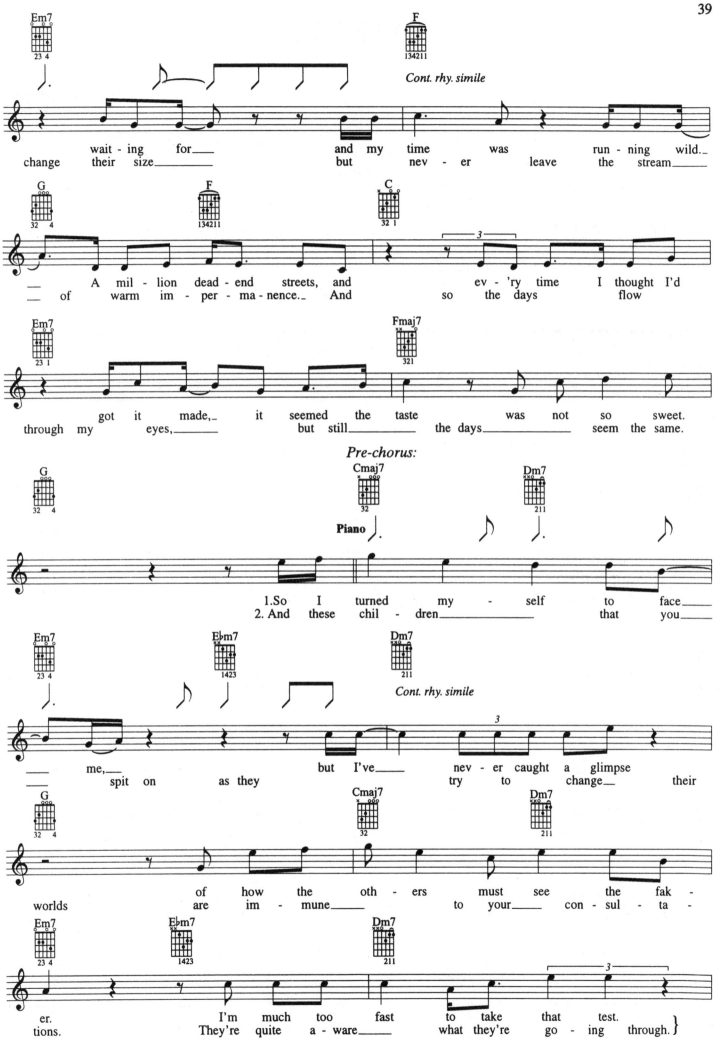

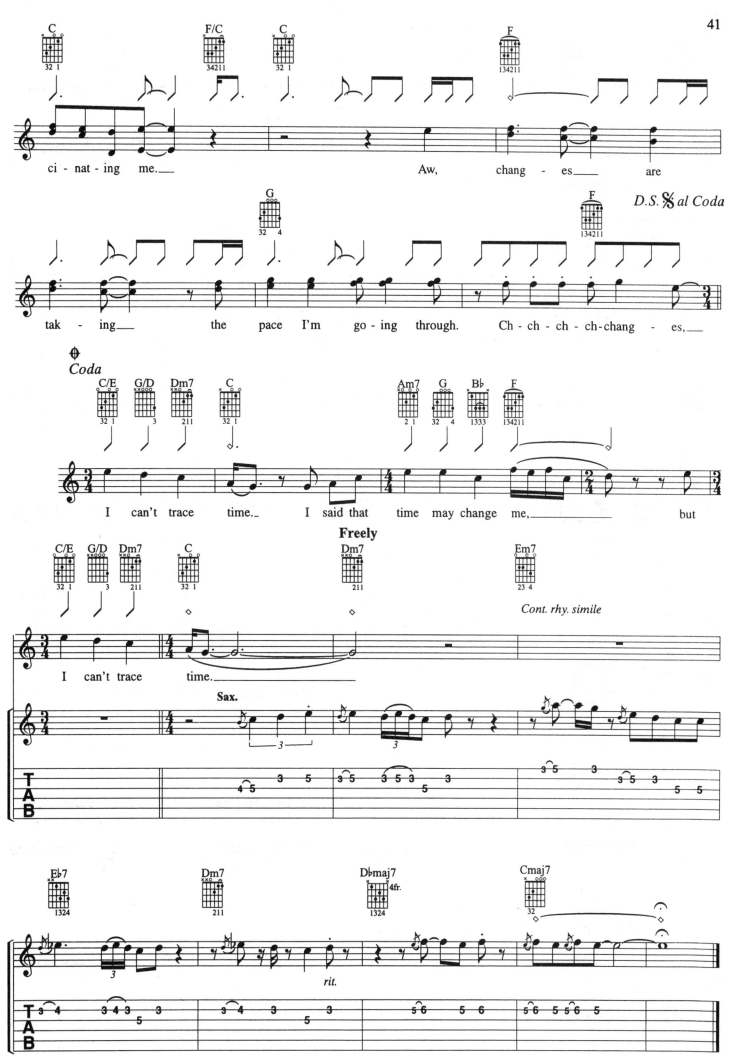

Changes - 4 - 4

COCAINE

Words and Music by
JOHN J. CALE

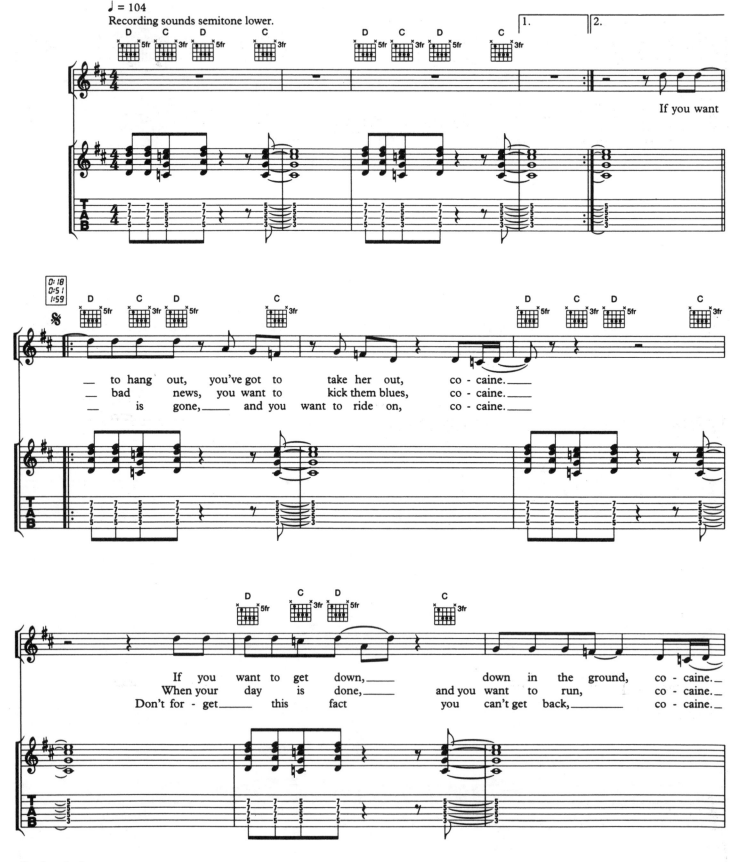

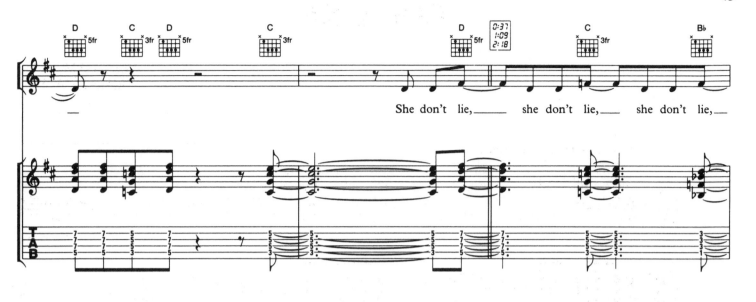

She don't lie,____ she don't lie,____ she don't lie,____

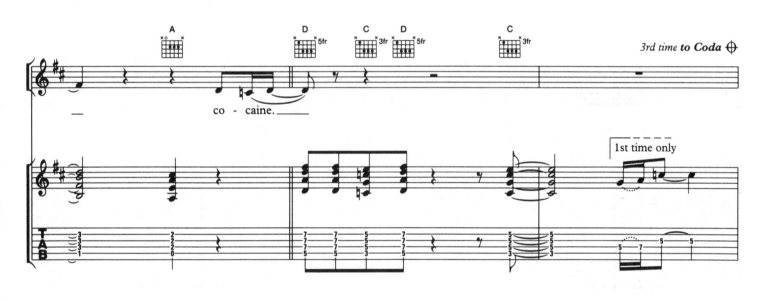

co - caine.____

3rd time **to Coda** ⊕

1st time only

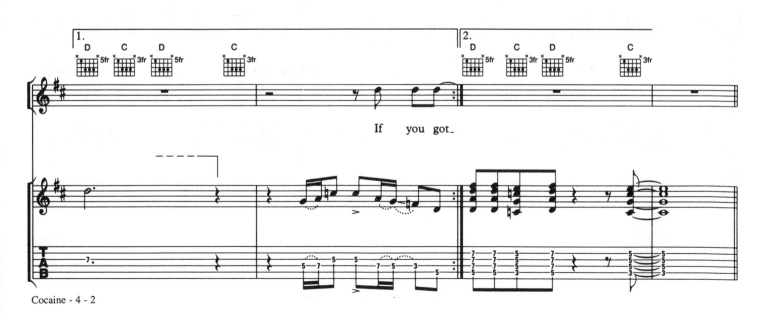

If you got_

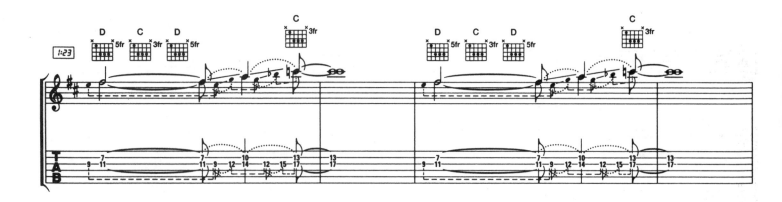

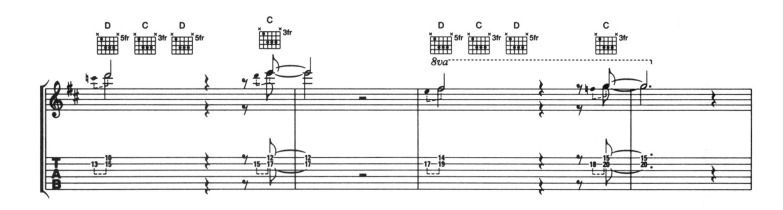

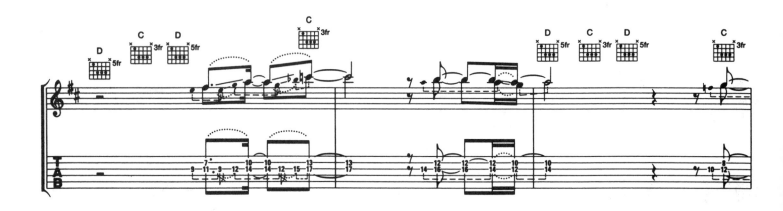

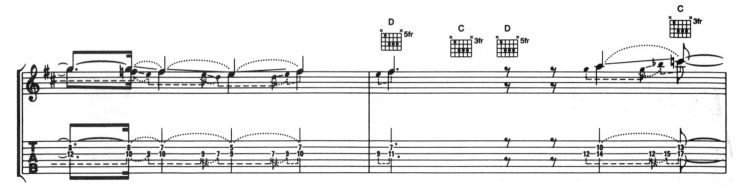

DANCE TO THE MUSIC

Words and Music by
SYLVESTER STEWART

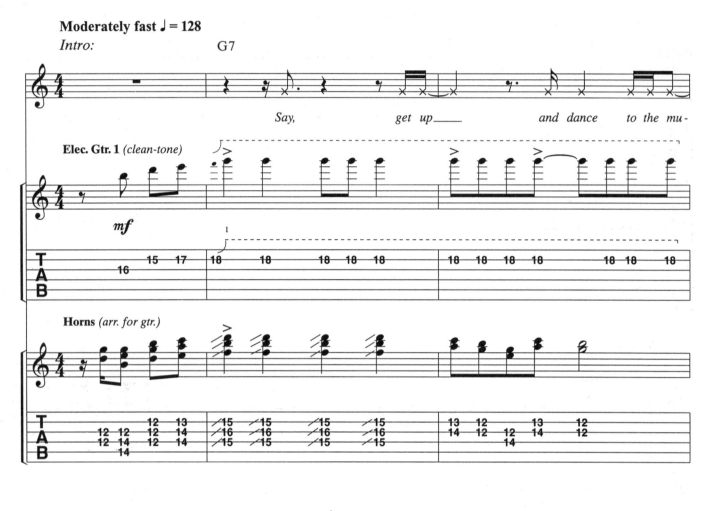

A capella

G7   C   G7

Do, do, do, do,— do, do, do, do, do, do,do, do, do,— do,do,do,
Do, do, do,do,do,do,do,do, do, do, do, do, do, do, do. do, do, do,—

Do, do, do, do, do, do, do, do, do, do, do, do, do, do,—

Chorus:
G   C 8fr.

do, do, do, do. Dance to the mu - sic,
— do, do, do.
— do, do, do.

Soprano Sax. *(arr. for gtr.)*

48

The dancers, they just won't hide.

You

Bass (arr. for gtr.)

Cont. simile

50

DOWN ON THE CORNER

Words and Music by
JOHN C. FOGERTY

start - ing to un - wind._ Four kids on the cor - ner trying to bring you up; _

Chorus:

Wil - ly picks _ a tune _ out and he blows it on the harp. Down on the cor - ner,

out here in the street, Wil - ly and the Poor - boys _ are playin'; _ bring a nick - el; tap your feet.

Interlude:

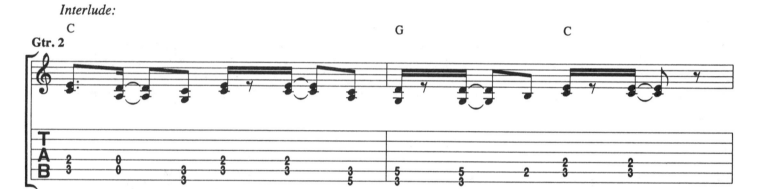

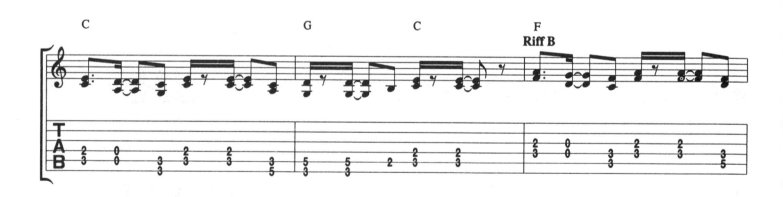

55

Verse 2:
Rooster hits the washboard,
People just gotta smile.
Blinky thumps the gut bass
And solos for a while.
Poor-boy twangs the rhythm out,
On his kalamazoo.
And Willy goes in to a dance
And doubles on kazoo.
(To Chorus:)

Down on the Corner - 3 - 3

EVIL WAYS

Words and Music by
SONNY HENRY

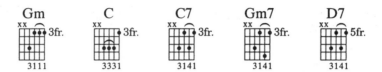

Moderate latin ♩ = 122

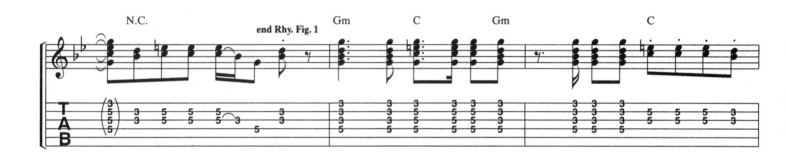

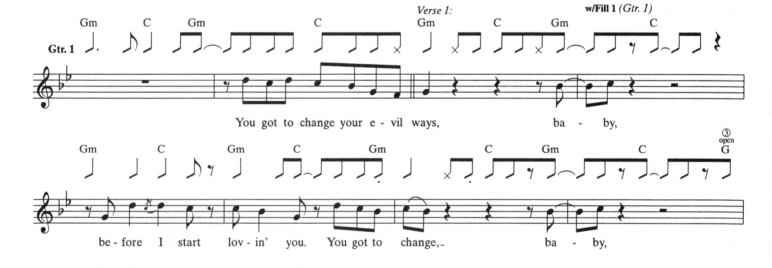

You got to change your e - vil ways, ba - by,

be - fore I start lov - in' you. You got to change,— ba - by,

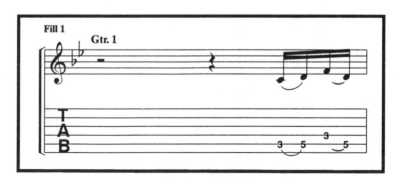

Evil Ways - 4 - 1

Evil Ways - 4 - 2

58

FREE BIRD

Words and Music by
ALLEN COLLINS and RONNIE VAN ZANT

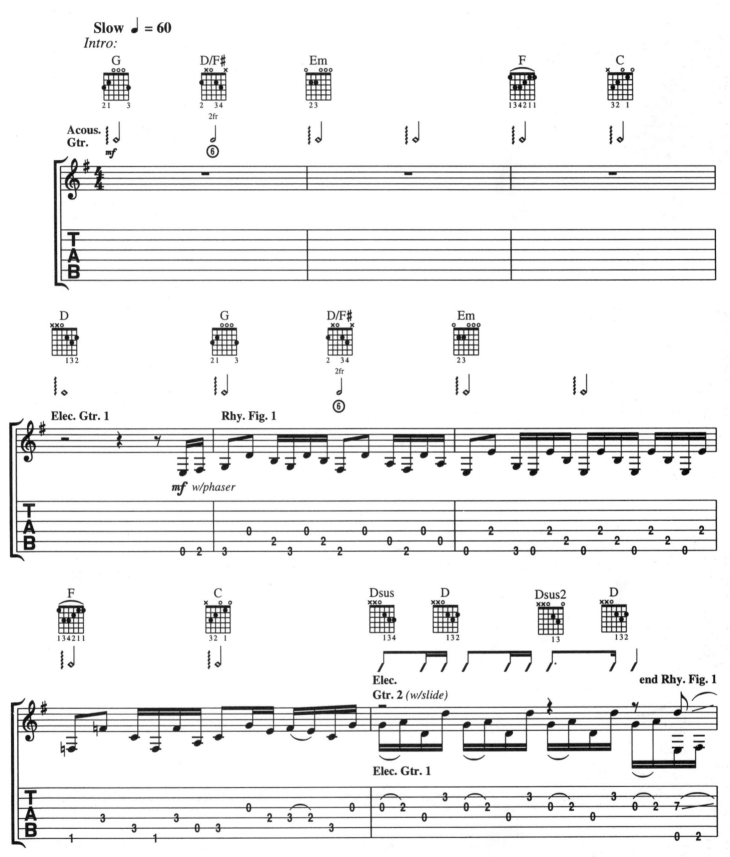

Free Bird - 9 - 1

61

Free Bird – 9 – 2

62

'Cause I'm as ___ free ___ as a bird ___ now, __

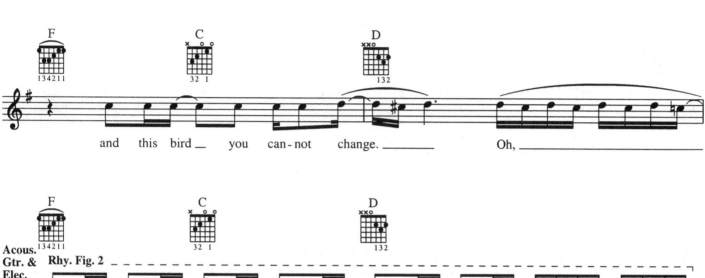

and this bird __ you can-not change. _____ Oh, _____

Acous. Gtr. & Elec. Gtr. 1

Rhy. Fig. 2

___ and the bird _ you can-not change, _____

w/Rhy. Fig. 2 *(Acous. Gtr. & Elec. Gtr. 1) 2 times*

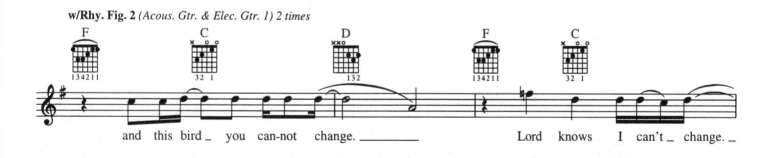

and this bird _ you can-not change. _____ Lord knows I can't _ change. _

1.
w/Rhy. Figs. 1 *(Elec. Gtr. 1)* **& 1A** *(Acous. Gtr.) both 2 times, simile*
w/Riff A *(Elec. Gtr. 2) simile*

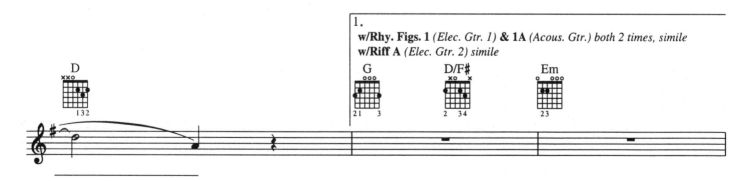

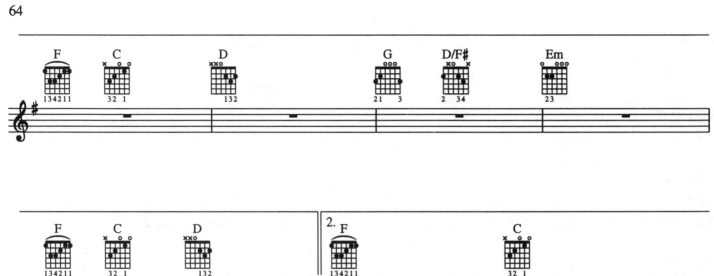

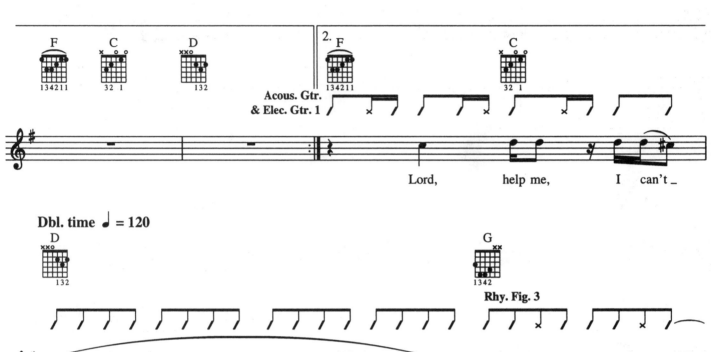

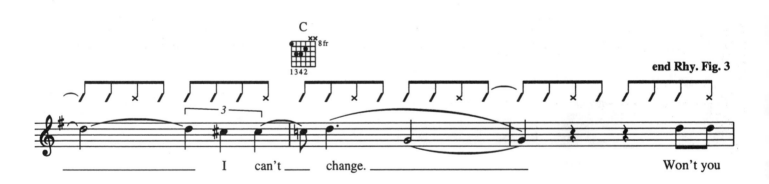

Free Bird – 9 – 5

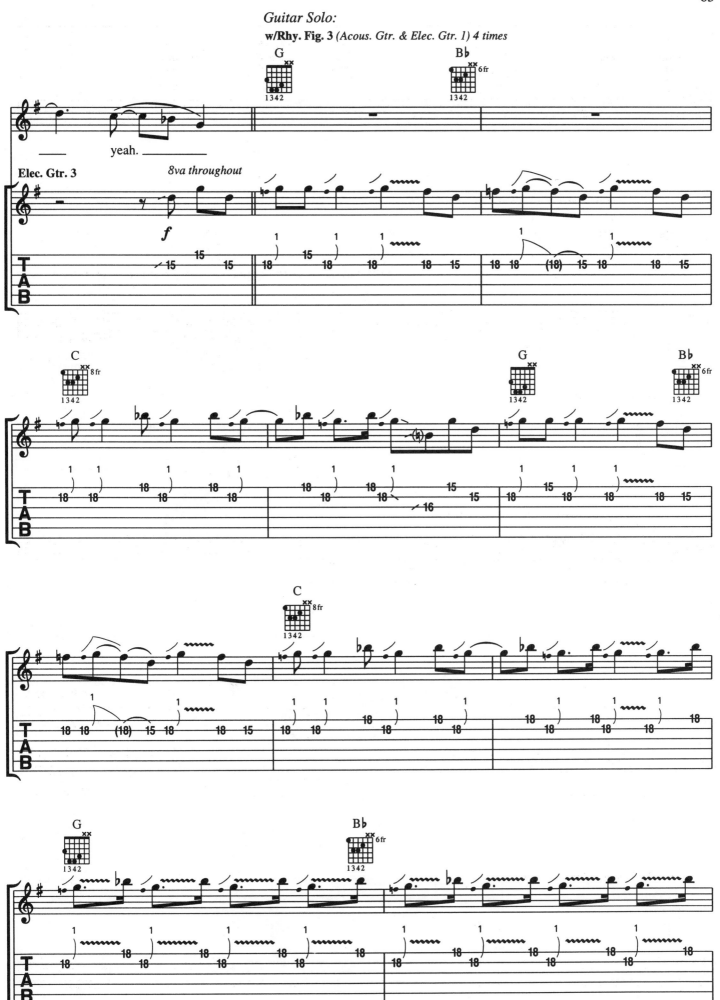

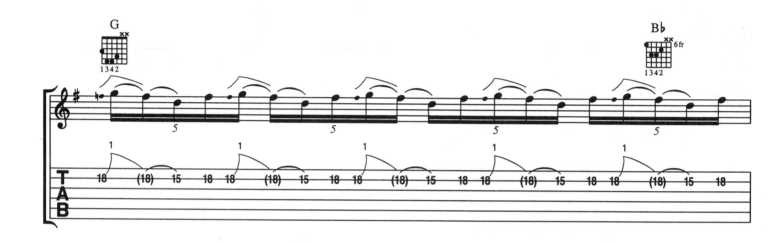

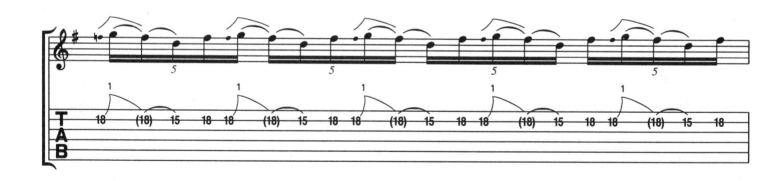

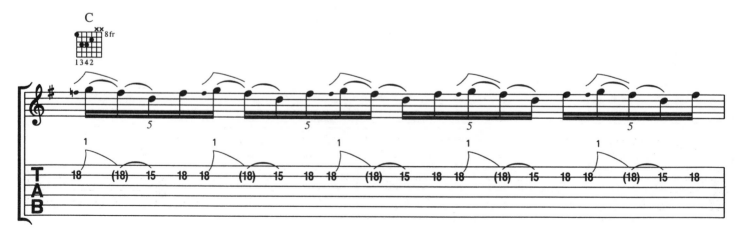

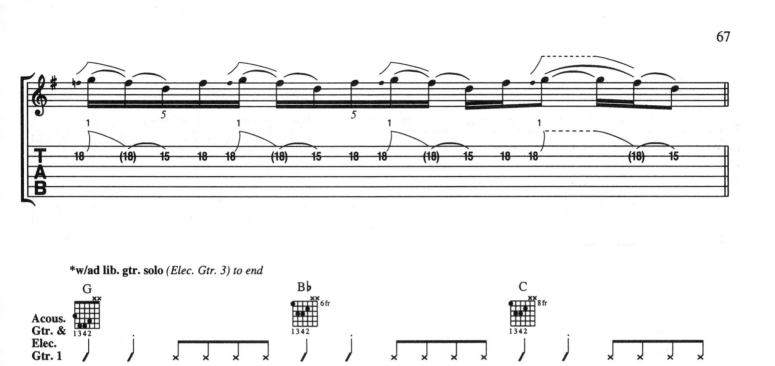

w/ad lib. gtr. solo (Elec. Gtr. 3) to end

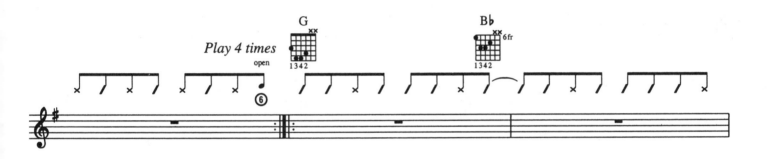

Ad lib. gtr. solo using G minor pentatonic scale (use previous 16 meas. as a model).

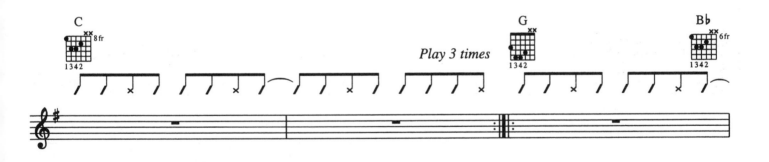

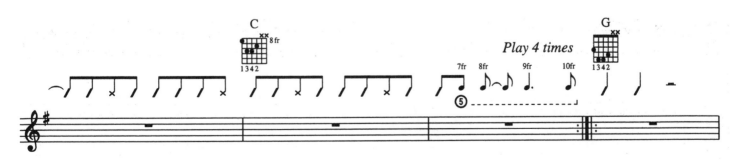

Free Bird – 9 – 8

HEART OF GOLD

Words and Music by
NEIL YOUNG

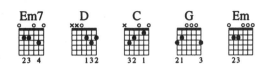

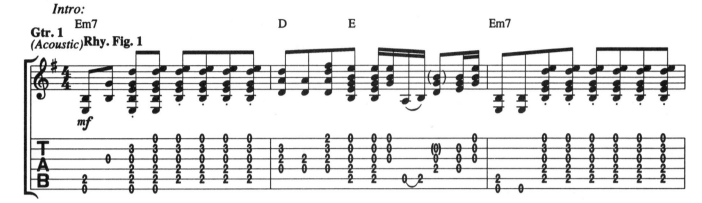

Moderately slow ♩ = 84

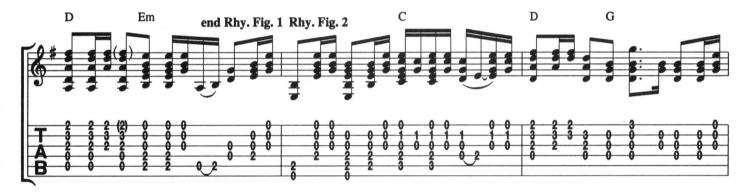

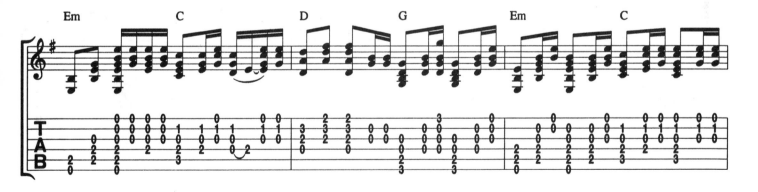

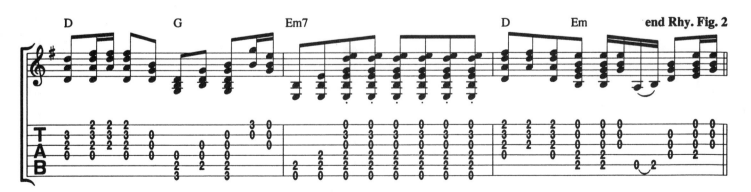

Heart of Gold - 3 - 1

70

Verse 2:
I've been to Hollywood, I've been to Redwood.
I cross the ocean for a heart of gold.
I've been in my mind, it's such a fine line
That keeps me searchin' for a heart of gold;
And I'm gettin' old.

A HORSE WITH NO NAME

Words and Music by
DEWEY BUNNELL

A Horse With No Name - 5 - 1

A Horse With No Name - 5 - 2

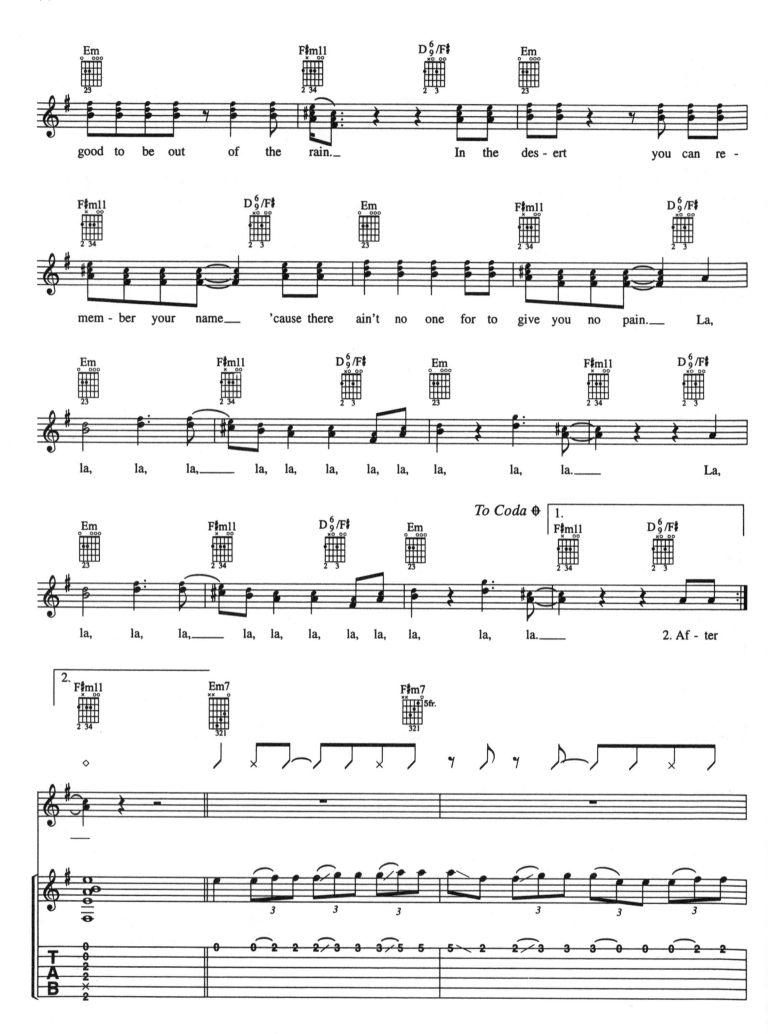

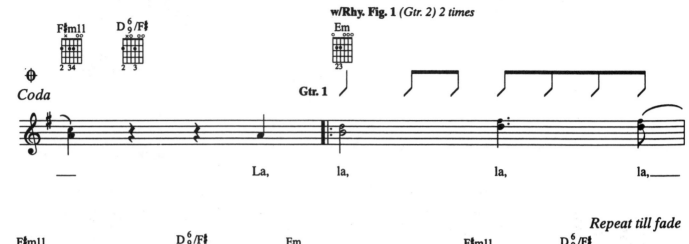

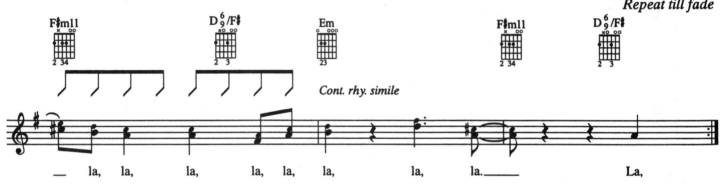

Verse 2:
After two days in the desert sun,
My skin began to turn red.
After three days in the desert fun,
I was looking at a river bed.
And the story it told of a river that flowed
Made me sad to think it was dead.
(To Chorus:)

Verse 3:
After nine days I let the horse run free
'Cause the desert had turned to sea.
There were plants and birds and rocks and things,
There was sand and hills and rings.
The ocean is a desert with its life underground
And a perfect disguise above.
Under the cities lies a heart made of ground,
But the humans will give no love.
(To Chorus:)

HOT FUN IN THE SUMMERTIME

Words and Music by
SYLVESTER STEWART

Chorus:

Hot fun in the sum - mer - time.___ Hot fun in the

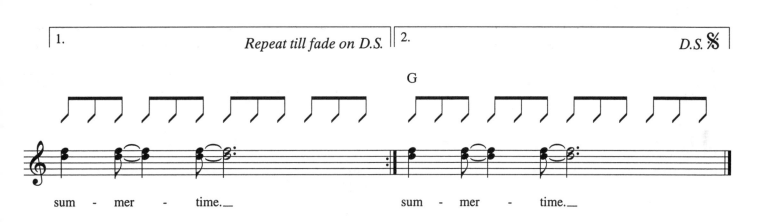

1. *Repeat till fade on D.S.* **2.** D.S. 𝄋

sum - mer - time.___ sum - mer - time.___

Verse 3:
First of the fall and then she goes back.
Bye, bye, bye, bye there.
Them summer days,
Those summer days.

Pre-chorus:
Boo, boo, boo, boo, boo when I want to.
Out of school.
County fair in the county sun.
And everything is cool.
Oh, yeah.
(To Chorus:)

I WANT TO TAKE YOU HIGHER

Words and Music by
SYLVESTER STEWART

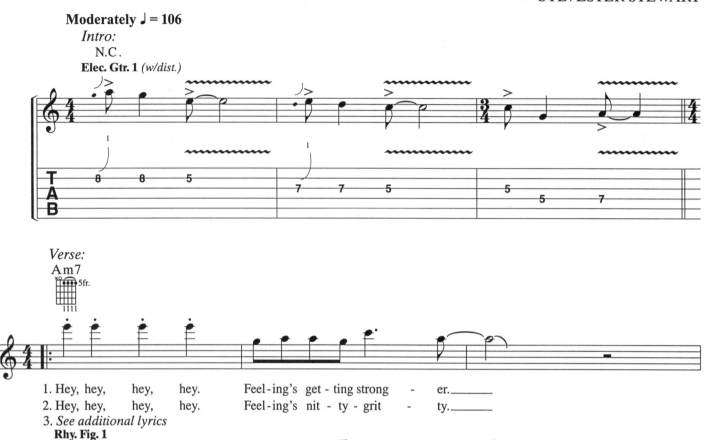

I Want to Take You Higher - 5 - 1

Chorus:

I want to, I want to, I want to take you high - er.
Don't ya, don't ya, don't, don't you want to get high - er?
Bkgd.Vcl.: High - er,

I want to take you high - er.
Don't ya want to get high - er?
high - er.

Ba - by, ba - by, ba - by, light my
Ba - by, ba - by, ba - by, light my

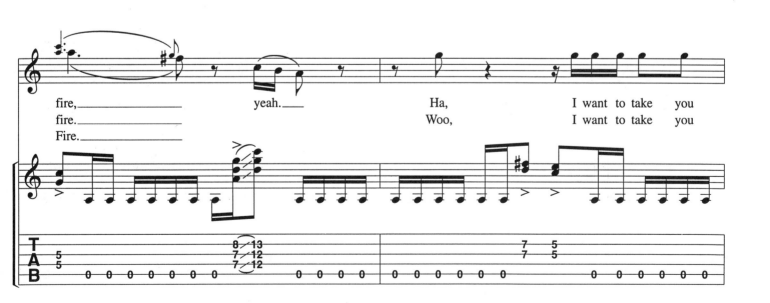

fire,_____ yeah.___ Ha, I want to take you
fire._____ Woo, I want to take you
Fire._____

high - er.
high - er.
High - er.

end Rhy. Fig. 2

Elec. Gtr. 1 tacet
N.C.

To Coda ⊕   *Interlude:*

Boom, la-ka, la-ka, la-ka, boom, la-ka, la-ka, la-ka.

Harmonica Solo:
w/**Rhy. Fig. 1** *(Elec. Gtr. 1) simile*
Am7

1.

2.

Hey, hey, hey, hey!

Vocal Fig. 1   **end Vocal Fig. 1**

Boom, la-ka, la-ka, la-ka, boom, la-ka, la-ka, la-ka, Boom, la-ka, la-ka, la-ka, boom, la-ka, la-ka, la-ka,

I Want to Take You Higher - 5 - 3

Boom, la - ka, la - ka, la - ka, boom, la - ka, la - ka, la - ka,   Boom, la - ka, la - ka, la - ka, boom, la - ka, la - ka, la - ka,

Chorus:
w/Rhy. Fig. 2 *(Elec. Gtr. 1) simile*

High - er, high - er, high - er, high - er, Won't you light my
high - er,

D.C. al Coda

fire.__ I want to take you high - er.__
high - er, high - er.

Guitar Solo:
w/Rhy. Fig. 1 *(Elec. Gtr. 1) simile*
w/Vocal Fig. 1, *8 times, simile*

Am7

Elec. Gtr. 2 *(w/dist.)*
Coda

Chorus:
w/Rhy. Fig. 2 *(Elec. Gtr. 1) simile*

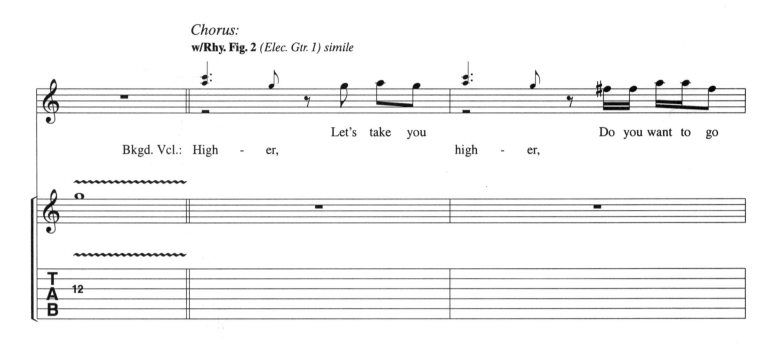

Let's take you — Do you want to go

Bkgd. Vcl.: High - er, high - er,

with me, babe? If you do won't you light my

high - er, high - er, high - er,

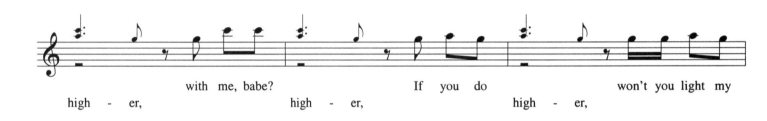

Repeat for trumpet, bass and sax solos ad lib. and fade

fire.___ Want to take you high - er.___

high - er, high - er, high - er.

Verse 3:
Feeling that could make you move.
Sounds that should help you groove.
Music still flashing me.
Take your places.
I want to take you higher
Baby, baby, baby, light my fire.
(To Chorus:)

LAYLA

Words and Music by
ERIC CLAPTON and JIM GORDON

Layla – 9 – 1

Layla – 9 – 3

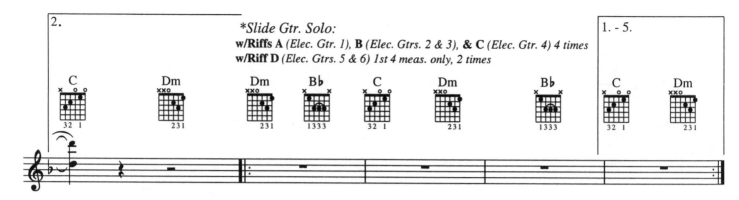

*w/ad lib. slide gtr. solo (D minor pentatonic scale).

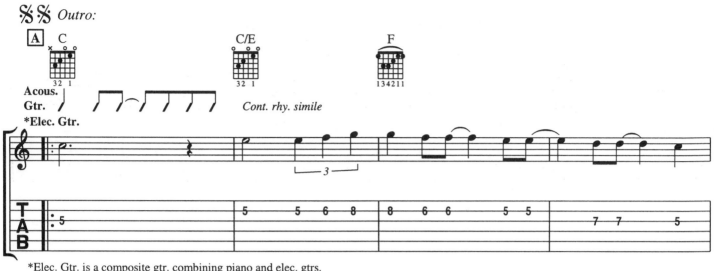

*Elec. Gtr. is a composite gtr. combining piano and elec. gtrs.

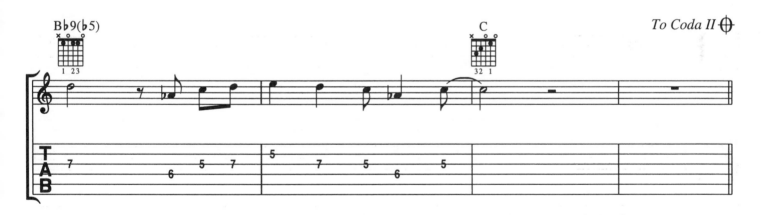

Layla – 9 – 7

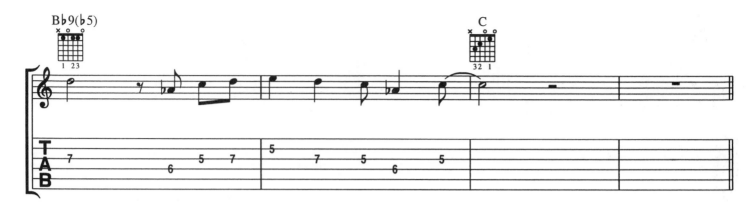

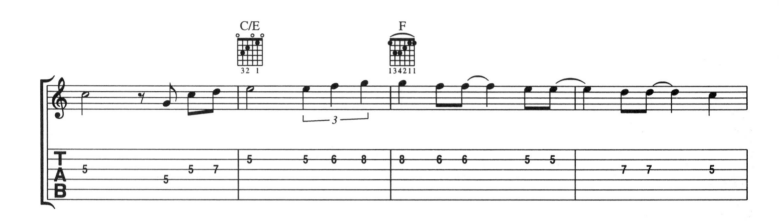

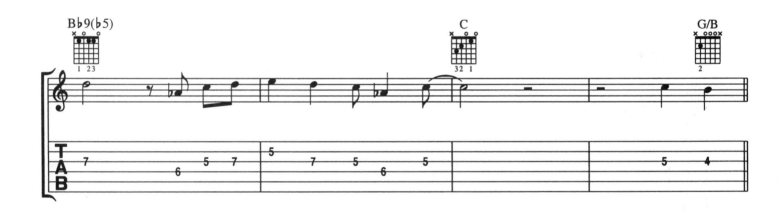

Layla – 9 – 8

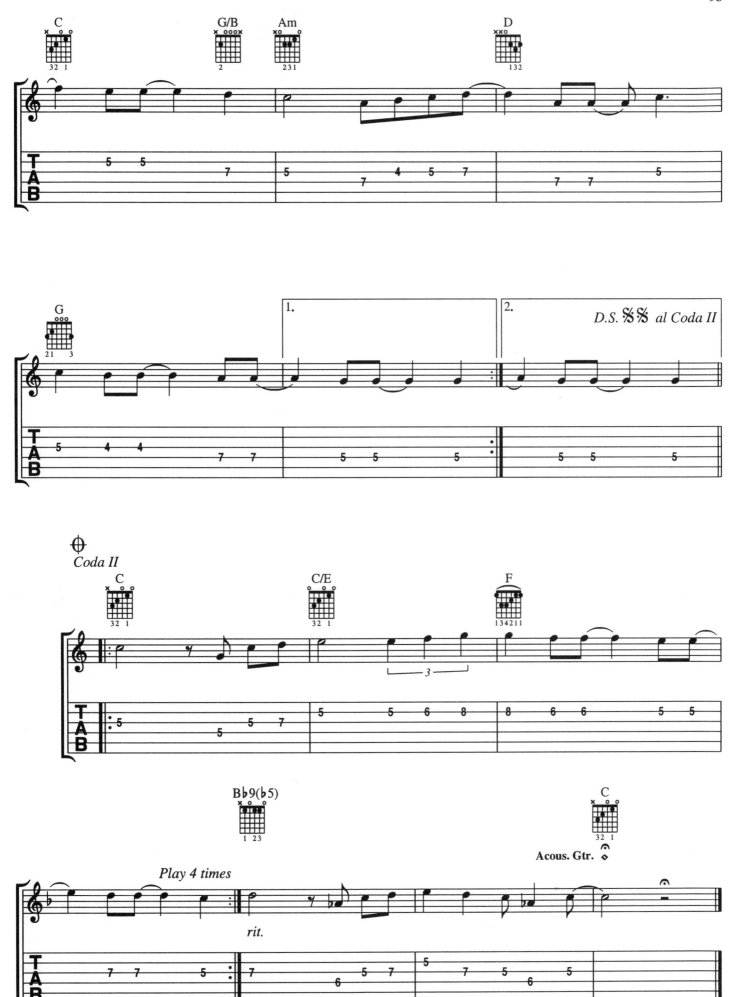

Layla – 9 – 9

THE LOW SPARK OF HIGH-HEELED BOYS

Words and Music by
STEVE WINWOOD and JIM CAPALDI

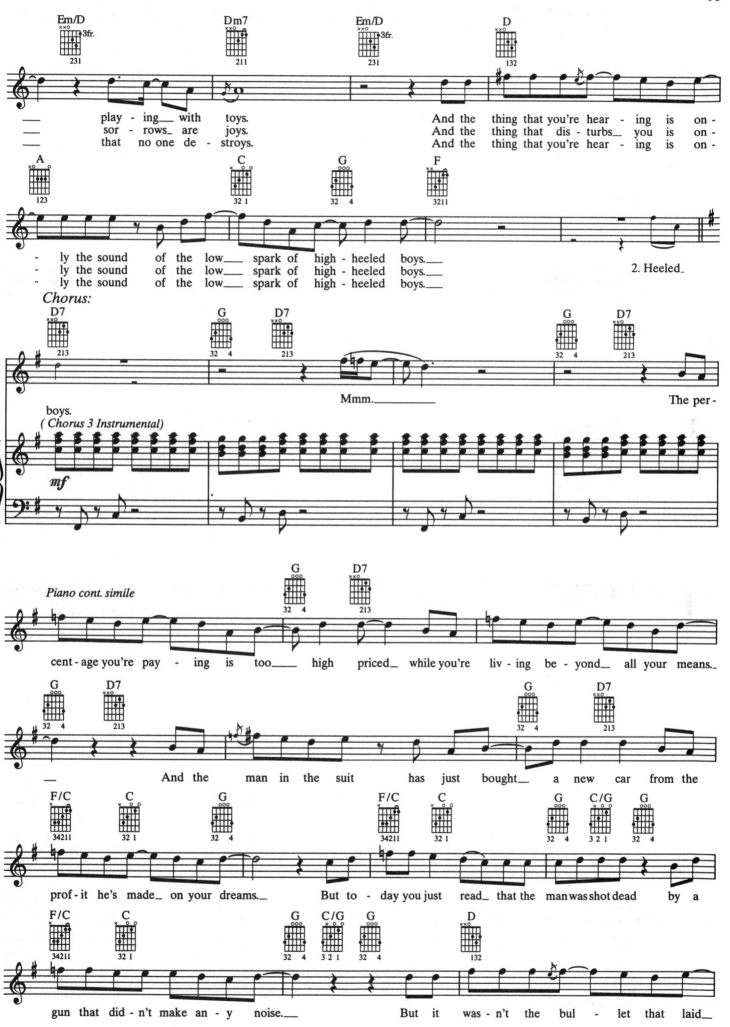

The Low Spark of High-Heeled Boys - 3 - 2

96

The Low Spark of High-Heeled Boys - 3 - 3

MAGGIE MAY

Words and Music by
ROD STEWART and MARTIN QUITTENTON

Moderate rock ♩ = 132
Intro:
Gtr. 1 (Acoustic 12-stg.)

Verse:

1. Wake up, Mag-gie, I ___ think I got some-thing to say to you. _ It's
2.-4. *See additional lyrics*

late Sep-tem-ber, and I real-ly should _ be back ___ at ___ school. I

know I keep you a-mused, ___ but I feel I'm be-ing used _____ ah. Oh,

Mag-gie I could-n't have tried ___ an-y more. _____ You

Maggie May - 3 - 1

98

led me a-way from ___ home   just to save you from be-ing a - lone.   You

stole my heart, ___ and that's ___   what real - ly hurts. ___

Guitar Solo:

Coda

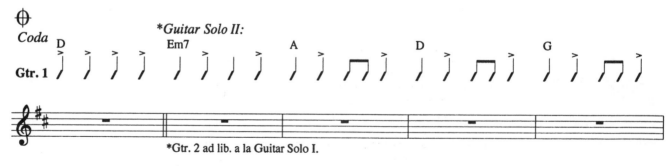

*Gtr. 2 ad lib. a la Guitar Solo I.

Maggie May - 3 - 2

*w/ad lib. lead vocal
on repeats.

Verse 2:
The morning sun, when it's in your face,
Really shows your age.
But that don't worry me none,
In my eyes you're everything.
I laughed at all of your jokes,
My love you didn't need to coax.
Oh, Maggie, I couldn't have tried anymore.
You lead me away from home just to save
You from being alone.
You stole my soul, and that's a pain
I could live without.

Verse 3:
All I needed was a friend to lend
A guiding hand.
But you turned into a lover, and
Mother, what a lover, you wore me out.
All you did was wreck my bed,
And then the morning kicked me in the head.
Oh, Maggie, I couldn't have tried anymore.
You lead me away from home 'cause you
Didn't want to be alone.
You stole my heart, I couldn't leave you if I tried.
(To Guitar Solo I:)

Verse 4:
I suppose I could collect my books
And get on back to school.
Or steal my daddy's cue, and make a living out of playing pool.
Or find myself a rock and roll band that needs a helping hand.
Oh Maggie, I wish I'd never seen your face.
You made a first-class fool out of me,
But I'm as blind as a fool can be.
You stole my heart, but I love you anyway.
(To Guitar Solo II:)

MACARTHUR PARK

Words and Music by
JIMMY WEBB

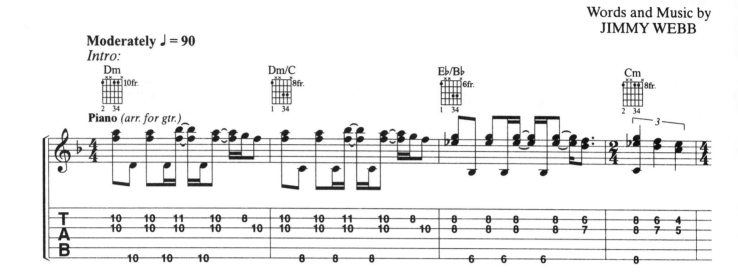

1. Spring was nev-er wait-ing____ for us, girl, it ran one step a-head____
2. I re-call the yel-low____ cot-ton dress foam-ing like a

MacArthur Park - 6 - 4

Double time

Instrumental Interlude:

MAMA TOLD ME (NOT TO COME)

Words and Music by
RANDY NEWMAN

Mama Told Me (Not to Come) - 4 - 2

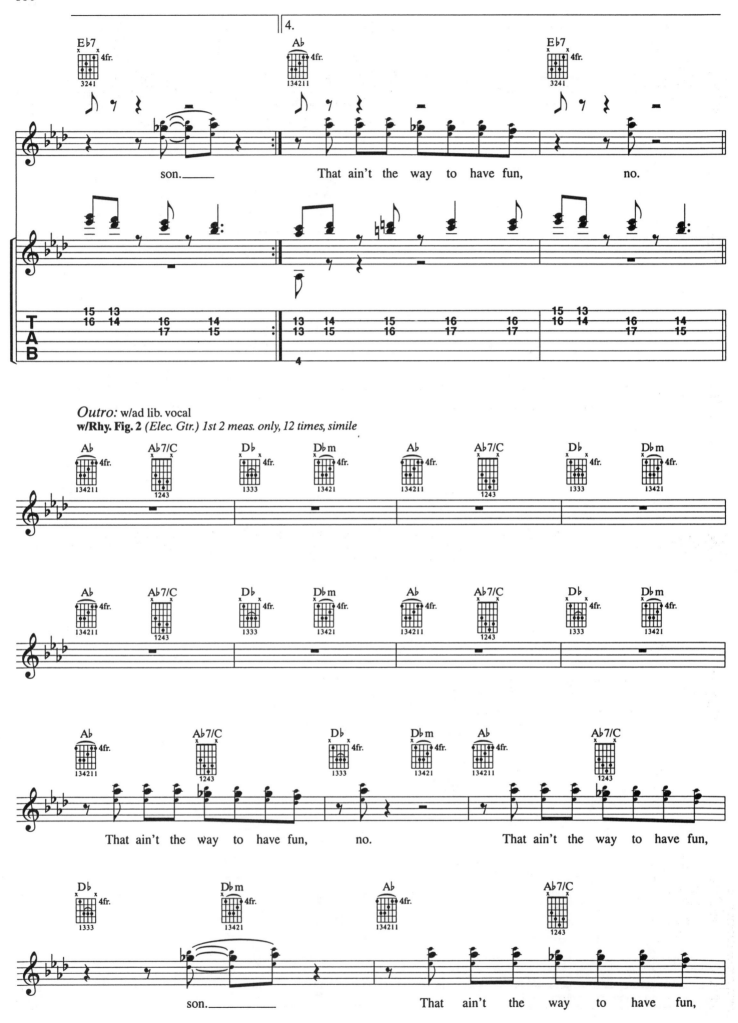

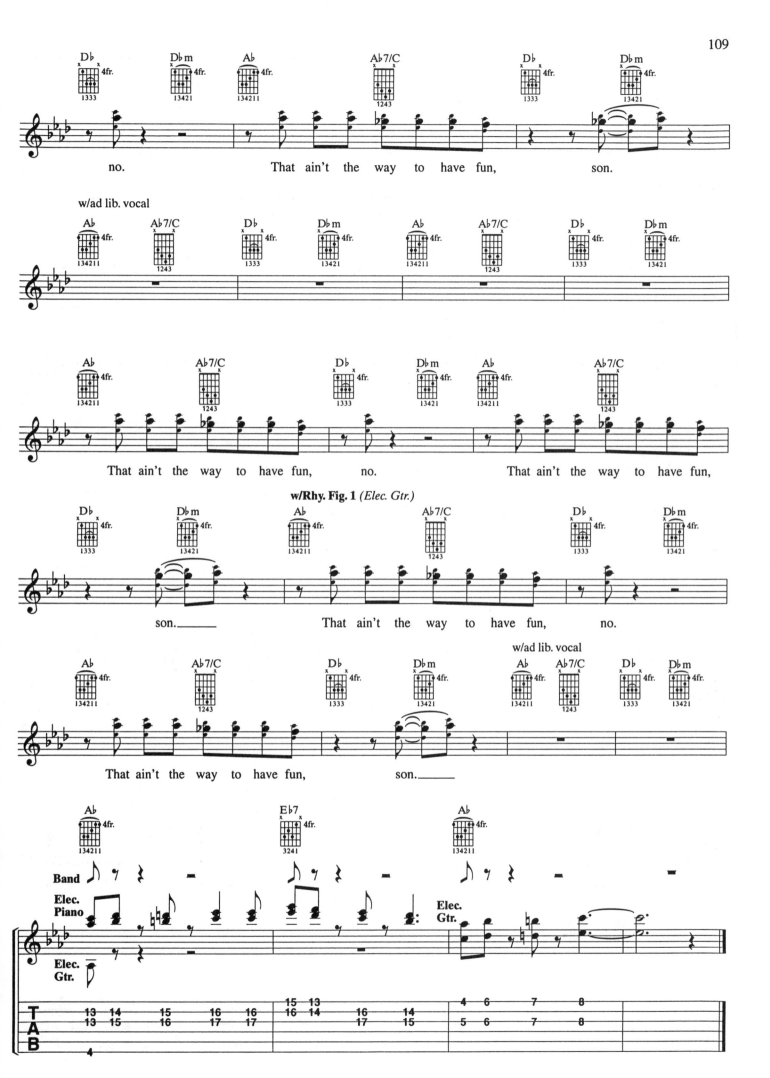

MAGIC CARPET RIDE

Words and Music by
RUSHTON MOREVE and JOHN KAY

I like to dream, yes,— yes, right be- tween the sound ma- chine.—

Magic Carpet Ride - 3 - 1

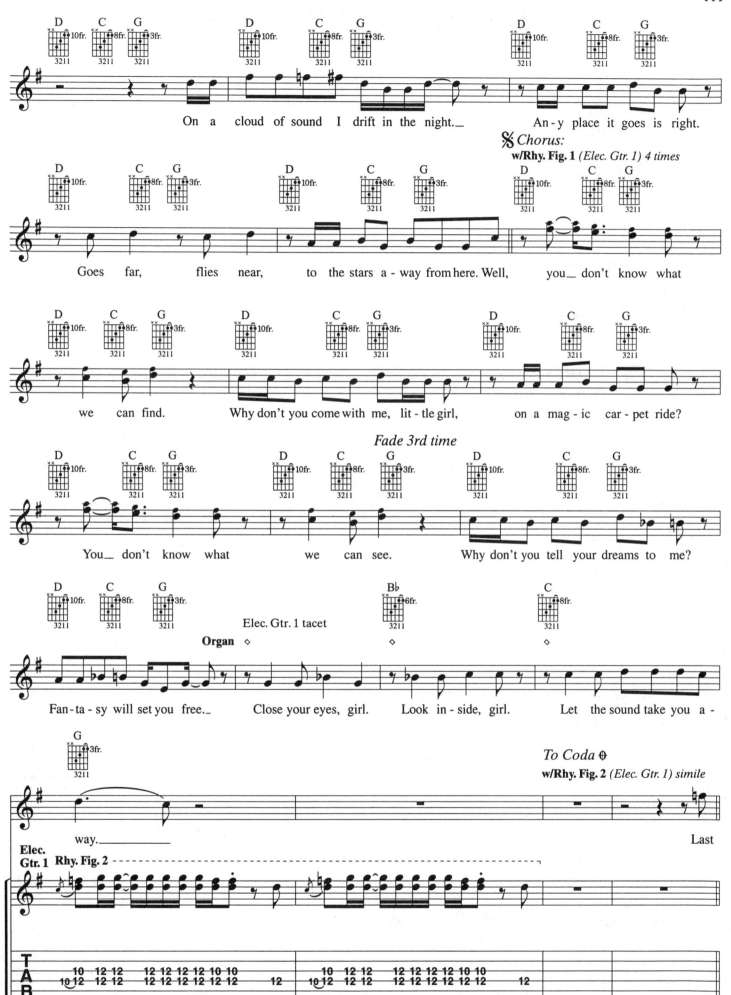

112

Verse 2:

w/Rhy. Fig. 1 *(Elec. Gtr. 1) 3 times*

night I held A - lad - din's lamp,___ and so I wished that I could stay.

Be - fore the thing could an - swer me, well, some - one came and took the lamp a - way.

D.S. % al Coda

I looked a - round, a lous - y can - dle's all I found. Well,

Coda

Elec. Gtr. 1

Double time (♩ = 216)

Interlude:

w/Rhy. Fig. 3 *(Elec. Gtr. 1)*
4 times

Rhy. Fig. 3 w/bkgd. noise & fdbk.

Play 51 times

Elec. Gtr. 2

w/slide

D.S. % and fade

MOONDANCE

Words and Music by
VAN MORRISON

Moondance - 5 - 1

114

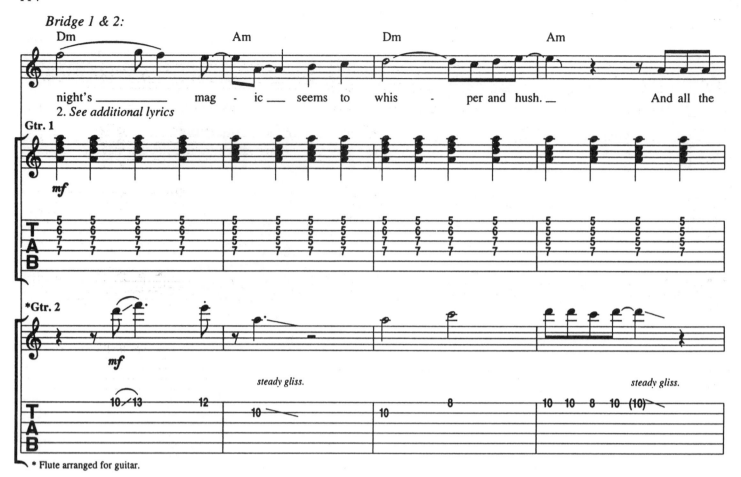

Bridge 1 & 2:

night's _____ mag - ic ____ seems to whis - per and hush. ___ And all the

2. *See additional lyrics*

Gtr. 1

*Gtr. 2

steady gliss.   *steady gliss.*

* Flute arranged for guitar.

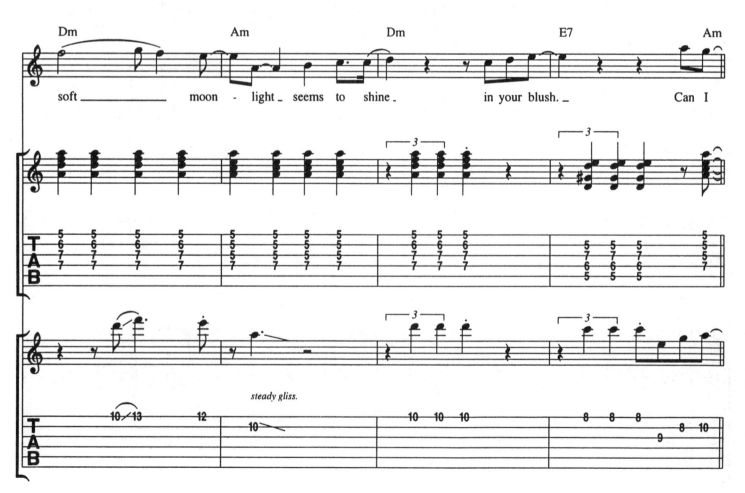

soft _____ moon - light _ seems to shine. _____ in your blush. ___ Can I

steady gliss.

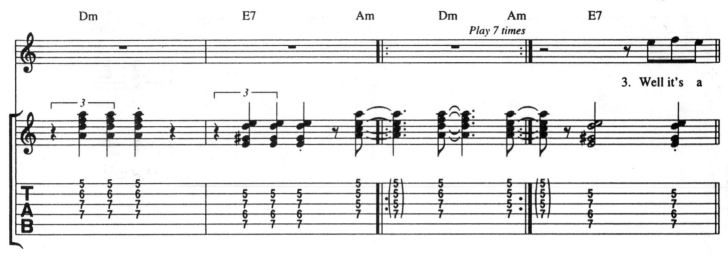

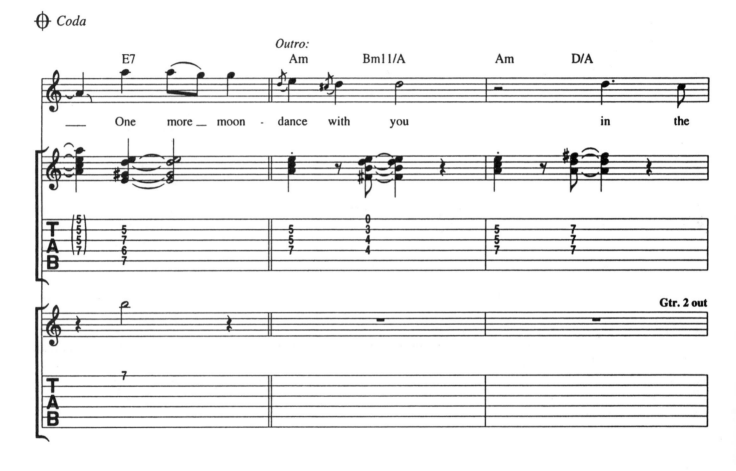

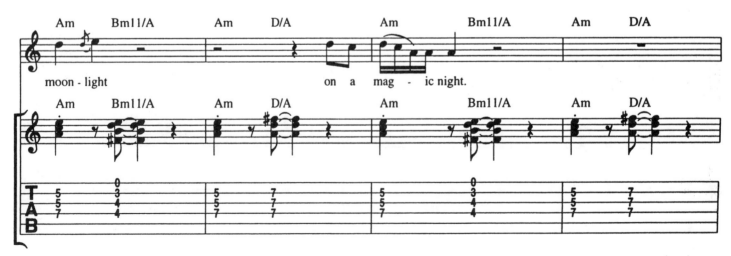

Verse 2:

Well I wanna make love to you tonight,
I can't wait 'til the morning has come.
And I know now the time is just right
And straight into my arms you will run.
And when you come, my heart will be waiting
To make sure that you're never alone.
There and then all my dreams will come true, dear,
There and then I will make you my own.

Bridge 2:

And everytime I touch you, you just tremble inside.
And I know how much you want me that you can't hide.

(To Chorus:)

HAVE YOU EVER SEEN THE RAIN?

Written by
J.C. FOGERTY

Have You Ever Seen the Rain? - 2 - 1

ny day,___ I know;___   shin - in' down___ like

Chorus:

wat - er.   I   want to

know,_____   have you ev - er_____   seen   the rain?

I   want to know,_____   have you ev - er_____   seen___   the

rain   com - in'   down___   on a sun - ny day?_

w/Rhy. Fill 1

2nd time only (Yeah!)   I   want to

know,___   have you ev - er _____ seen ___   the rain?

I   want to know, _____   have you ev - er_____   seen   the

rain   com - in'   down ___   on a sun - ny day?_

Verse 2:
Yesterday, and days before,
Sun is cold and rain is hard.
I know, been that way for all my time.

'Til forever, on it goes
Through the circle, fast and slow,
I know, and I can't stop. I wonder.

NIGHTS IN WHITE SATIN

Words and Music by
JUSTIN HAYWARD

121

Nights in White Satin - 3 - 2

Spoken: *Breathe deep, the gathering gloom,*
Watched lights fade from every room.
Bedsitter pensive people look back and lament,
Another day's useless, energy spent.
Impassioned lovers, wrestle as one
Lonely man cries for love and has none.
New mother picks up and suckles her son,
Senior citizens wish they were young.
Cold hearted orb that rules the night,
Removes the colors from our sight.
Red is gray, and yellow white,
But we decide which is right,
And which is an illusion.

OHIO

Words and Music by
NEIL YOUNG

Ohio - 11 - 1

126

Ohio - 11 - 4

128

130

should 've been done   long a go.   What if you knew   her and

found   her dead on the ground?   How could you run   when you know?

132

four dead in O - hi - o, four dead in O - hi - o, four dead in O - hi - o,

Fade out

four dead in O - hi - o, four dead in O - hi - o...

OLD MAN

Words and Music by
NEIL YOUNG

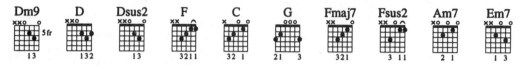

Slowly ♩ = 70

Intro :

Old man, look at my life, —

I'm a lot like you were. _____ Old man,

136

Old Man - 4 - 3

Chorus:

w/Rhy. Fig. 2 *(Gtr. 1, 3 times, simile)*

Old man, take a look at my life, _ I'm a lot ___ like _ you. ___ I ___ need

some-one to love _ me the whole _ day _ through. ___ Ah, ___ one

look, in my eyes _ an' you can tell that's _ true. ___

D.S. 𝄋 al Coda

Oo. ___

Coda
Gtr. 1

Verse 2:
Lullabies look in your eyes, run around the same old town.
Doesn't mean that much to me to mean that much to you.
I've been first and last, look at how the time goes past.
But I'm all alone at last, rolling home to you.
(To Chorus :)

PIECE OF MY HEART

Words and Music by
BERT BERNS and JERRY RAGAVOY

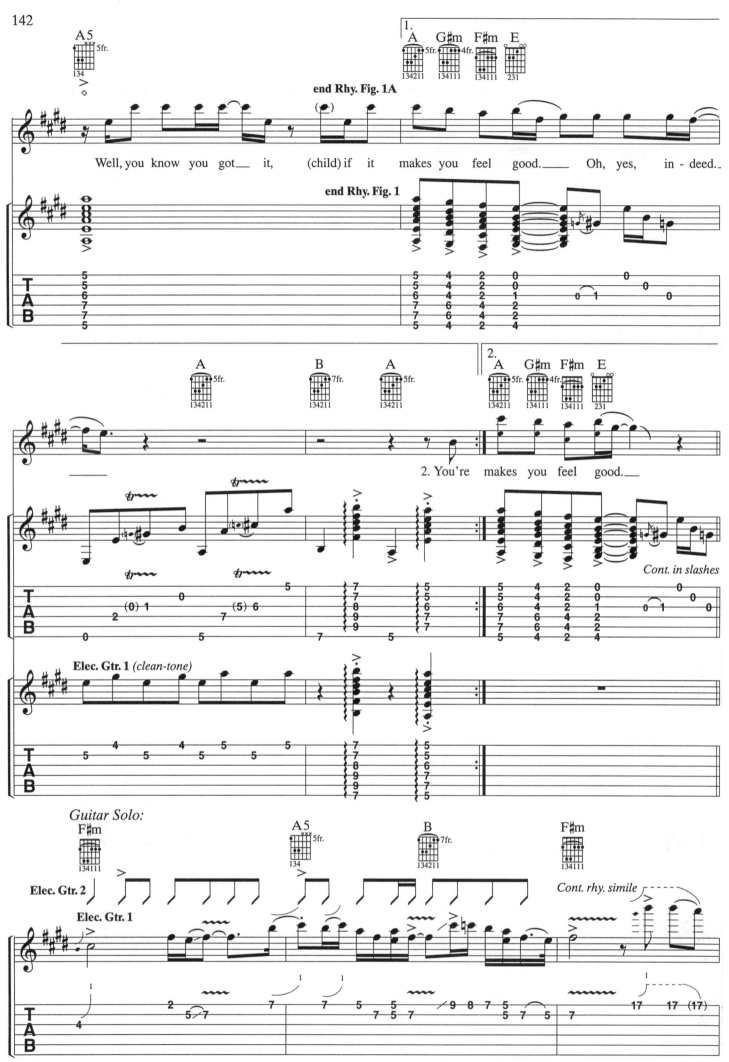

I need you to come___ on, come___ on, come on, come on and

Chorus:
w/Rhy. Figs. 1 *(Elec. Gtr. 2)* **& 1A** *(Elec. Gtr. 1) simile*

take it.   Take an-oth-er lit-tle piece of my heart___ now, ba - by.___
                                                        Bkgd. Vcl.: Oh,   oh,

break it!   Break an-oth-er lit-tle bit of my heart___ now, dar - lin' Yeah,_ yeah, yeah.___
                                                                                Oh,   oh,

have a...   Have an-oth-er lit-tle piece of my heart___ now, ba - by.___   You know you got_ it.   Whoa!_

Elec. Gtr. 1   **Elec. Gtr. 1**
                                                                                Cont. in notation

Well, you know you got_ it,   child, if it makes you feel good.___

Outro:

Elec. Gtr. 2
                                                                        rit.

Elec. Gtr. 1

                                                                        rit.

PROUD MARY

Words and Music by
J.C. FOGERTY

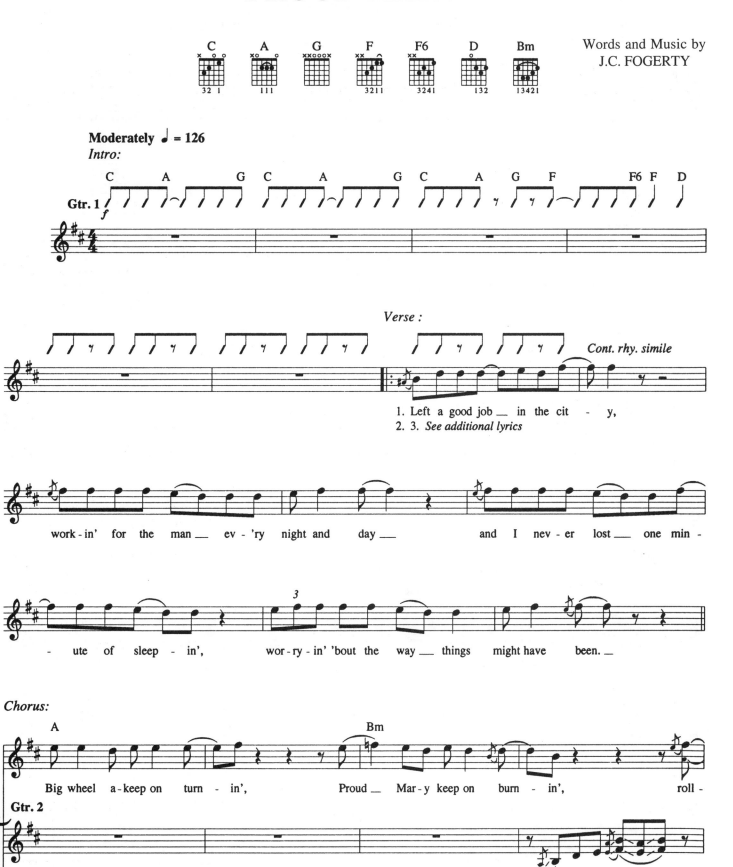

Proud Mary - 3 - 1

Verse 2:
Cleaned a lot of plates in Memphis,
Pumped a lot of pain down in New Orleans.
But I never saw the good side of the city
Till I hitched a ride on a river boat queen.
(To Chorus:)

Verse 3:
If you come down to the river,
Bet you're gonna find some people who live.
You don't have to worry
'Cause you have no money,
People on the river are happy to give.
(To Chorus:)

ROCK AND ROLL ALL NITE

Tune Down 1/2 Step
①- Eb ④- Db
②- Bb ⑤- Ab
③- Gb ⑥- Eb

Words and Music by
PAUL STANLEY and GENE SIMMONS

Intro

Anthem Rock ♩ = 138

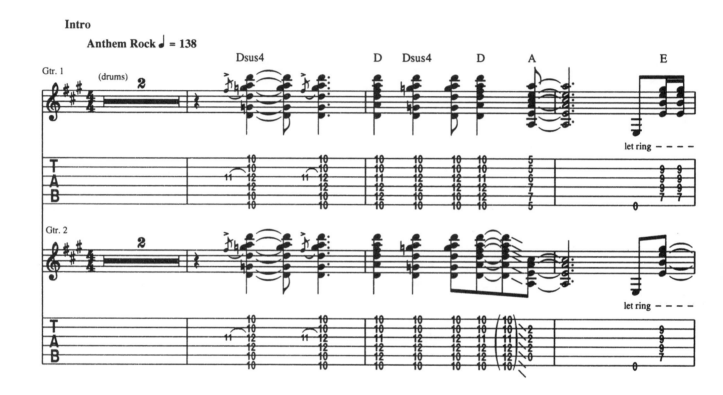

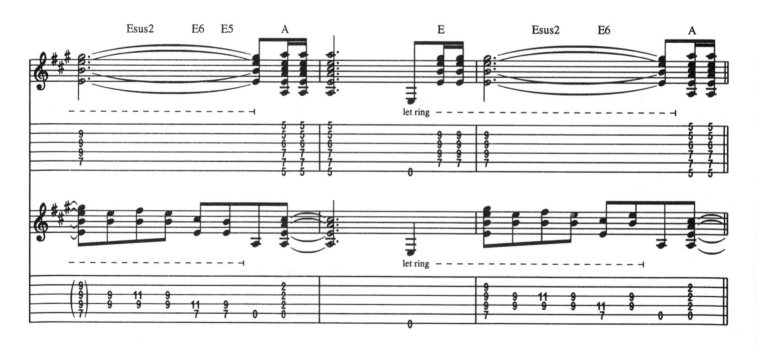

Rock and Roll All Nite - 9 - 1

Verse

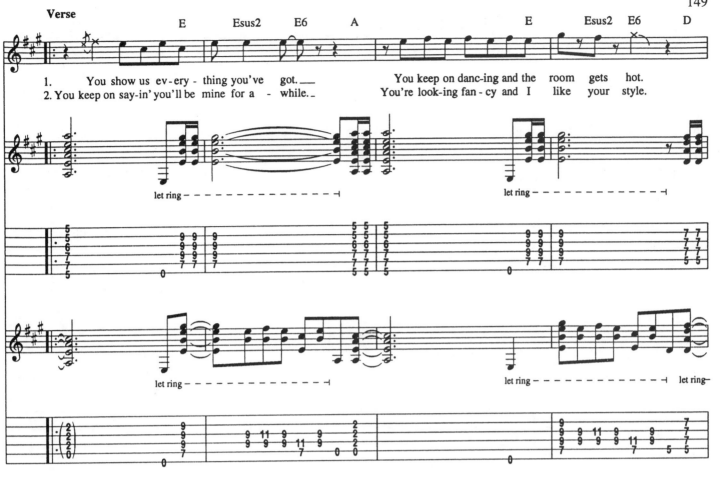

1. You show us ev-ery-thing you've got.___ You keep on danc-ing and the room gets hot.
2. You keep on say-in' you'll be mine for a - while.___ You're look-ing fan-cy and I like your style.

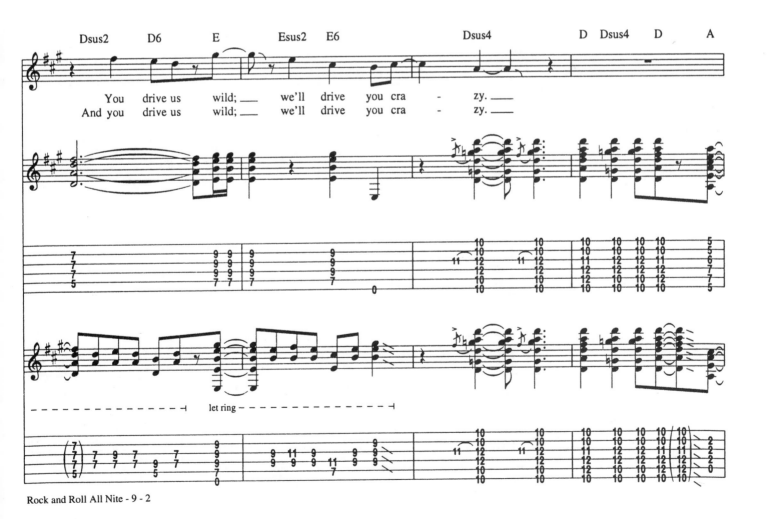

You drive us wild; ___ we'll drive you cra - zy. ___
And you drive us wild; ___ we'll drive you cra - zy. ___

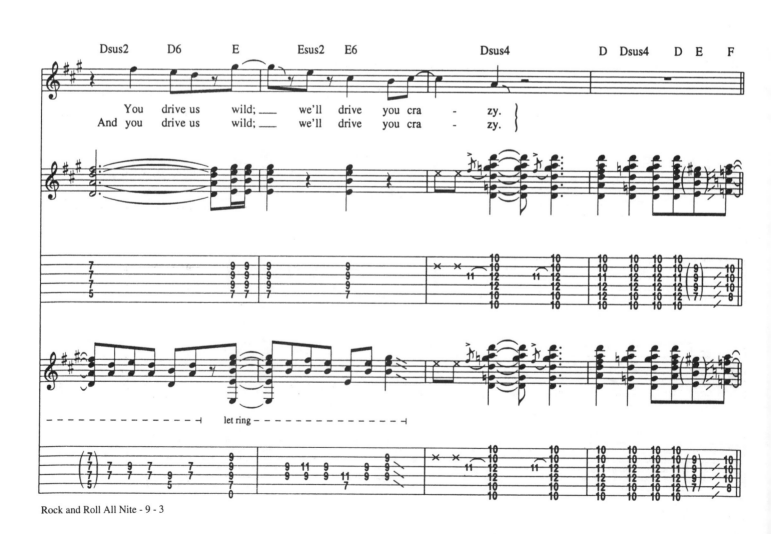

Rock and Roll All Nite - 9 - 3

Pre-Chorus

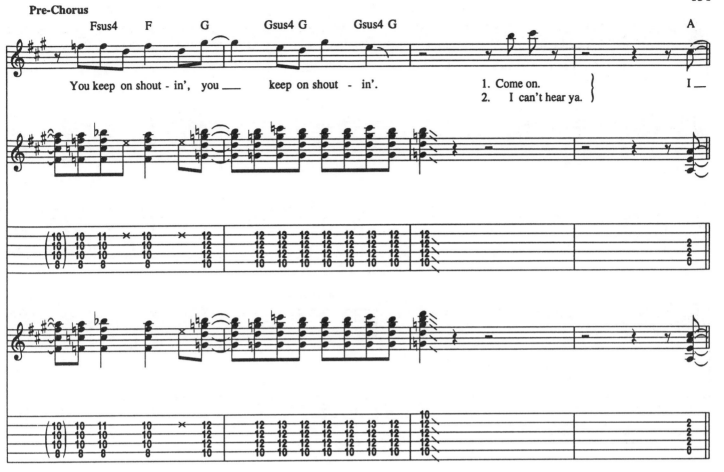

You keep on shout-in', you ___ keep on shout - in'.

1. Come on.
2. I can't hear ya.

I ___

Chorus

___ wan-na rock and roll ___ all night, _____ and par-ty ev - ery day.

P.M. - - - - - - - - -

Rock and Roll All Nite - 9 - 4

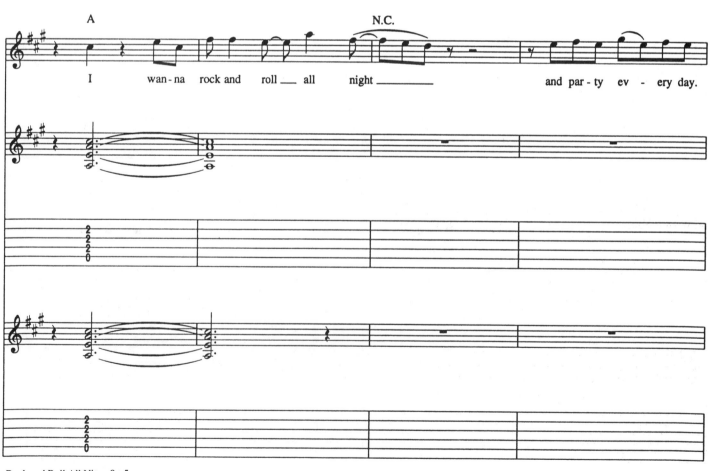

154

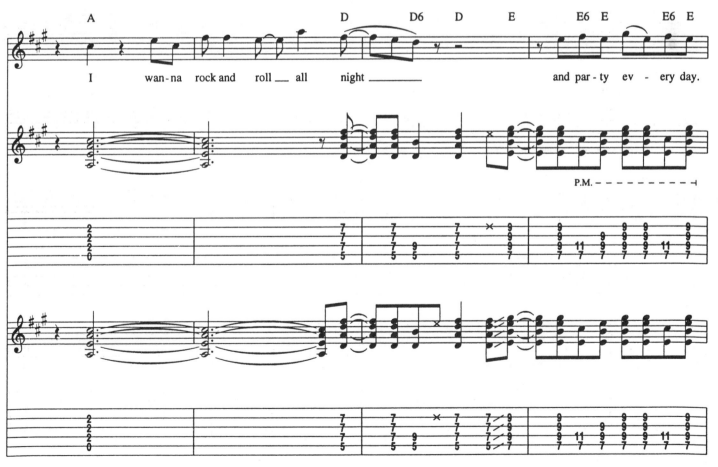

Rock and Roll All Nite - 9 - 8

156

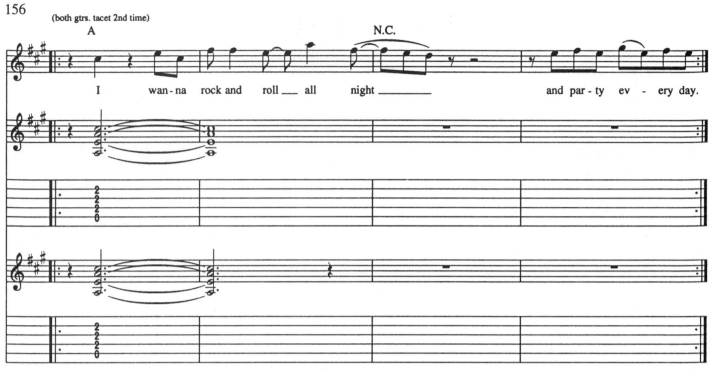

I wan-na rock and roll __ all night __ and par-ty ev - ery day.

Outro

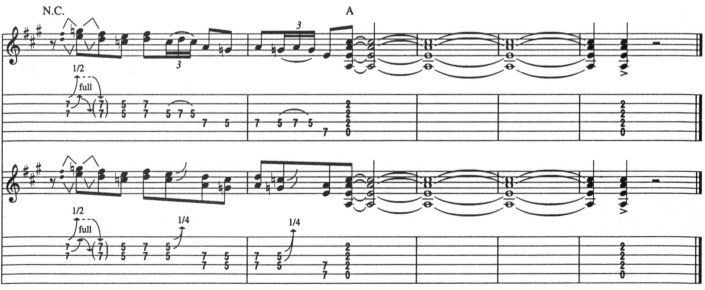

Rock and Roll All Nite - 9 - 9

ROCKET MAN
(I Think It's Gonna Be a Long Long Time)

Words and Music by
ELTON JOHN and BERNIE TAUPIN

*To match key of recording, capo 1st fret.

1. She packed my bags last night pre-flight.
2. Mars ain't the kind of place to raise your kids.

Ze-ro hour, nine A. M.
In fact, it's cold as hell.

And I'm gon-na be high as a kite by then.
And there's no one there to raise them if you did.

I miss the earth so much. I miss my wife.
And all this sci-ence I un-der-stand.

Rocket Man - 4 - 1

158

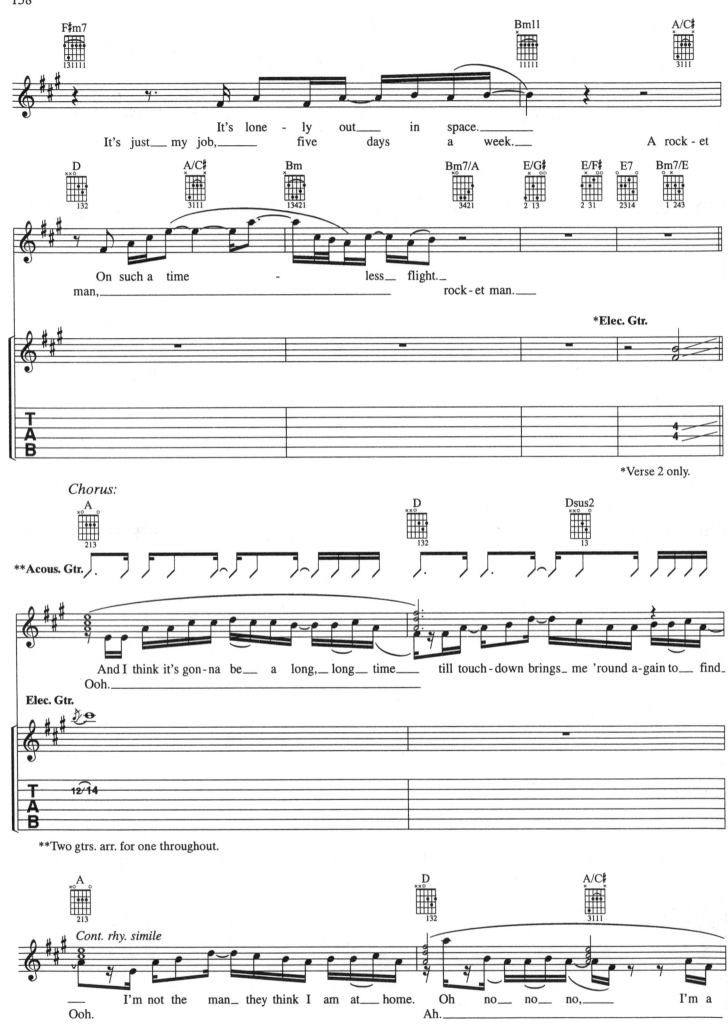

*Elec. Gtr.

*Verse 2 only.

Chorus:

**Acous. Gtr.

Elec. Gtr.

**Two gtrs. arr. for one throughout.

Cont. rhy. simile

It's lone - ly out___ in space._____
It's just___ my job,_____ five days a week._____ A rock - et

On such a time - less___ flight.___
man,_____ rock - et man.___

And I think it's gon-na be___ a long,___ long___ time____ till touch-down brings_ me 'round a-gain to___ find___
Ooh._____

___ I'm not the man___ they think I am at___ home. Oh no___ no___ no,_____ I'm a
Ooh. Ah.____

STOP DRAGGIN' MY HEART AROUND

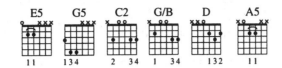

Words and Music by
TOM PETTY and MIKE CAMPBELL

Stop Draggin' My Heart Around - 3 - 1

Chorus:

Ba - by you could nev - er look me in the eye. ___

___ Yeah, you'd buck - le with the weight of the world. __ Stop drag - gin' my,

stop drag - gin' my, stop drag - gin' my heart a - round.

To Coda ⊕

Interlude:

w/Rhy. Fig. 1 (1st 2 bars)

Rhy. Fig. 3

(end Rhy. Fig. 3)

hold -

w/Rhy. Fig. 3 (2 times)

w/Rhy. Fig. 1
w/Fill 1 *(see page 1)*

D.S. 𝄋 *al Coda*

Ooh. ___

⊕ *Coda* w/Rhy. Fig. 1

w/Fill 2 *(see page 1)*

Repeat and fade

Stop drag- gin' my heart ___ a - round. ___

(vocal tacet 1st time)

Verse 3:
There's people runnin' 'round loose in the world.
Ain't got nothin' better to do
Than make a meal out of some bright-eyed kid.
You need someone looking after you.
I know you really want to tell me goodbye.
I know you really want to be your own girl.
(To Chorus:)

Stop Draggin' My Heart Around - 3 - 3

SUFFRAGETTE CITY

Words and Music by
DAVID BOWIE

Moderately fast ♩ = 144

*Two Elec. Gtrs. & Acous. Gtr.
arr. for one Elec. Gtr. throughout.

1. Aw, leave me a - lone,___ you know.
2. My school day's in - sane.___
3. Oh Hen - ry, don't be un - kind,___ go 'way.

Hey, man.___

Woah, Hen - ry, get off the phone.___ I got to,
My work's down the drain___
I can't take___ her this time,___ no way.___

Hey, man.___

SUNSHINE OF YOUR LOVE

Words and Music by
JACK BRUCE, PETE BROWN
and ERIC CLAPTON

To Coda ⊕

Gtr. 1: w/ Rhy. Fill 1, 2nd & 3rd times

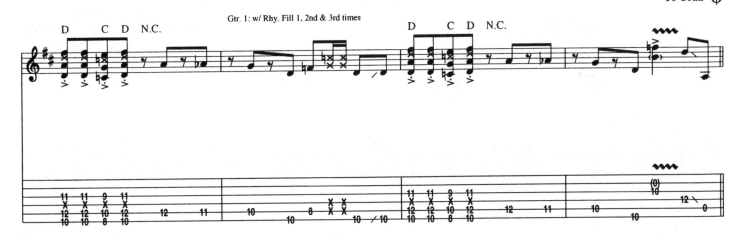

Chorus

I've __ been wait - ing so __ long   to __ be where __ I'm go - ing

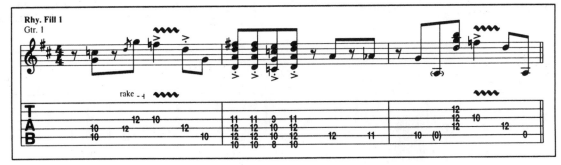

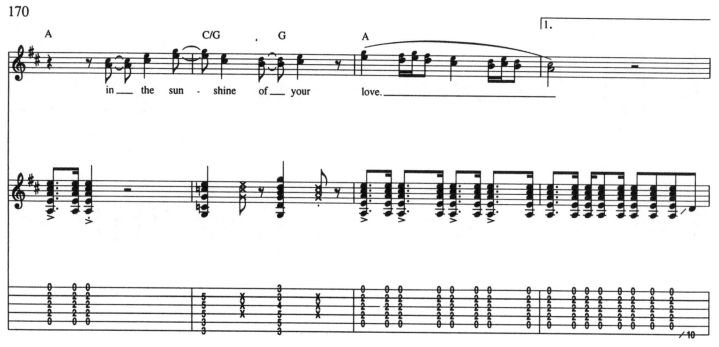

in __ the sun - shine of __ your love. _____

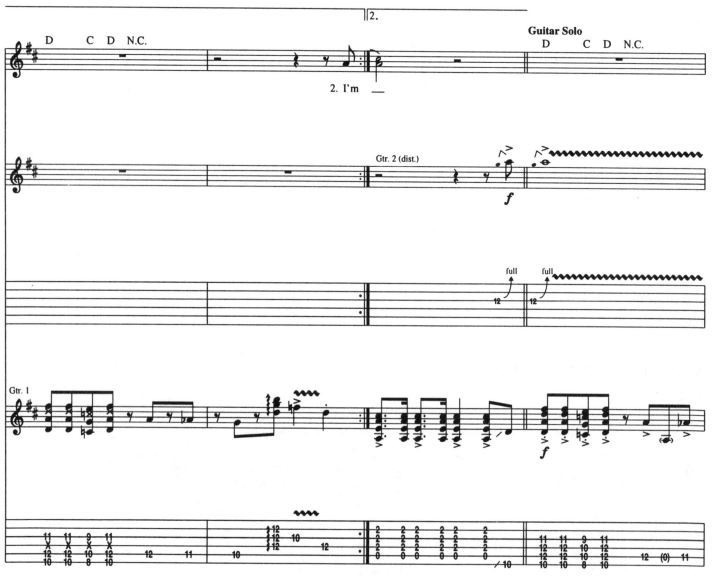

2. I'm __

Guitar Solo

Gtr. 2 (dist.)

Gtr. 1

Sunshine of Your Love - 6 - 4

D.S. al Coda
(2nd lyrics)

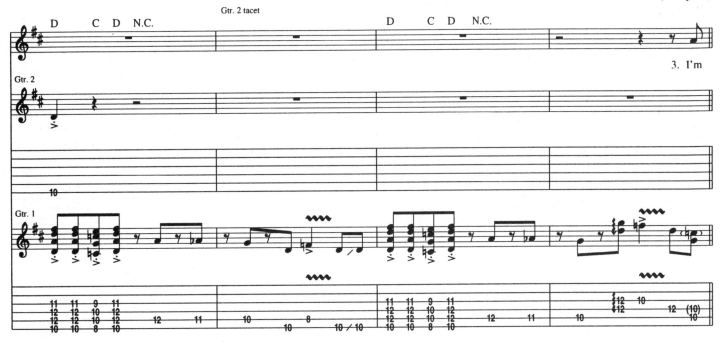

3. I'm

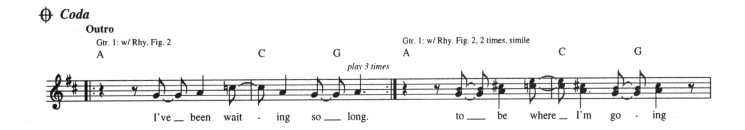

⊕ *Coda*

Outro

I've __ been wait - ing so __ long.   to __ be where __ I'm go - ing

in __ the sun - shine of __ your   love. _____

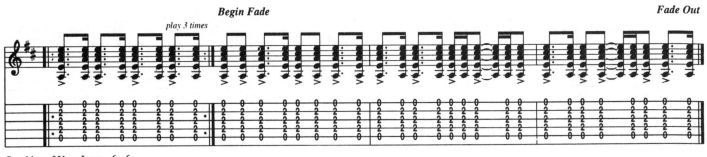

Sunshine of Your Love - 6 - 6

SWEET HOME ALABAMA

Words and Music by
RONNIE VAN ZANT, ED KING
and GARY ROSSINGTON

*Depress and release trem. bar at each beat indicated

Verse

Gtr. 1: w/ Rhy. Fig. 1
Gtr. 2: w/ Riff A, 1 3/4 times

2. Well, I heard Mist-er Young sing a-bout __ her.   Well, I heard old Neil ___ put 'er down.
(Ooh,   ooh,   ooh.   Ooh,   ooh,

Sweet Home Alabama - 8 - 2

Guitar Solo

Gtr. 1: w/ Rhy. Fig. 4

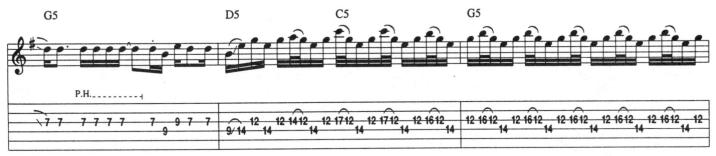

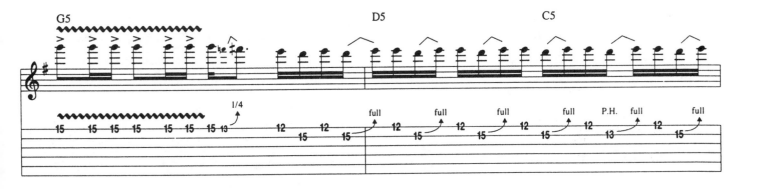

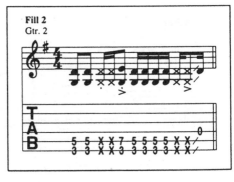

Ah,   ah,   ah,   Al-a-bam-a!

Sweet Home Alabama - 8 - 6

bam - a, where the skies are so blue.___

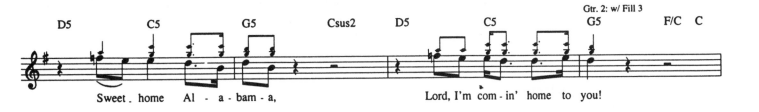

Sweet _ home Al - a - bam - a, Lord, I'm com - in' home to you!

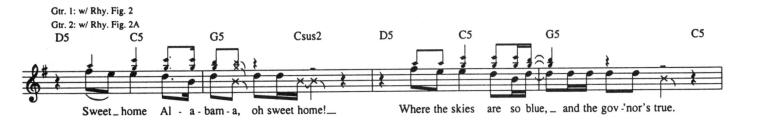

Sweet _ home Al - a - bam - a, oh sweet home!___ Where the skies are so blue, _ and the gov.'nor's true.

Sweet _ home Al - a - bam - a, oh ___ yeah. Lord, I'm com in' - home to you. Yeah. ___
(Oo! Oo! Oo!)

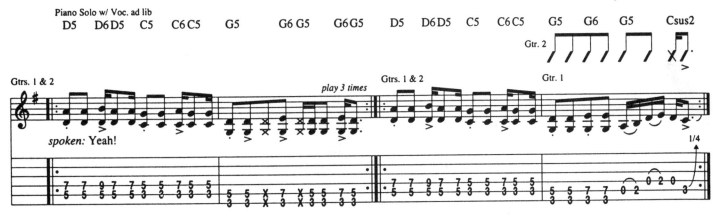

TAKE IT EASY

Words and Music by
JACKSON BROWNE and GLENN FREY

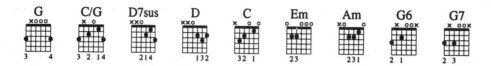

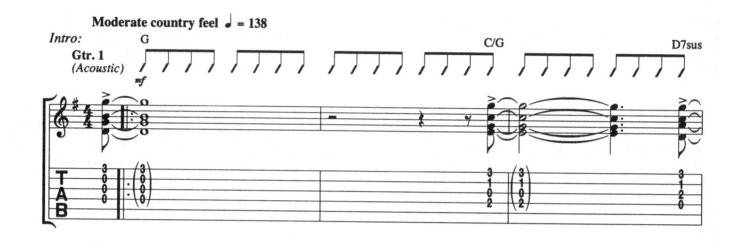

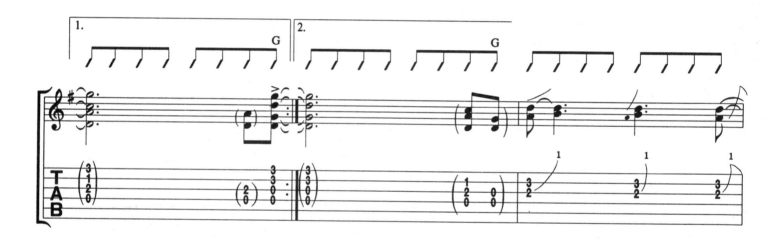

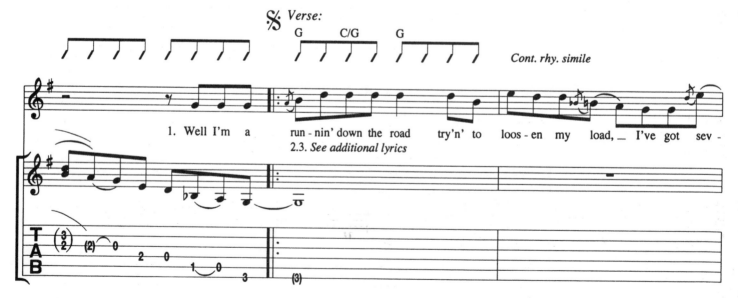

1. Well I'm a run-nin' down the road try'n' to loos-en my load, __ I've got sev-

2.3. *See additional lyrics*

Take It Easy - 4 - 1

*Substitute w/Am, Verse 3 only.

Take It Easy - 4 - 2

185

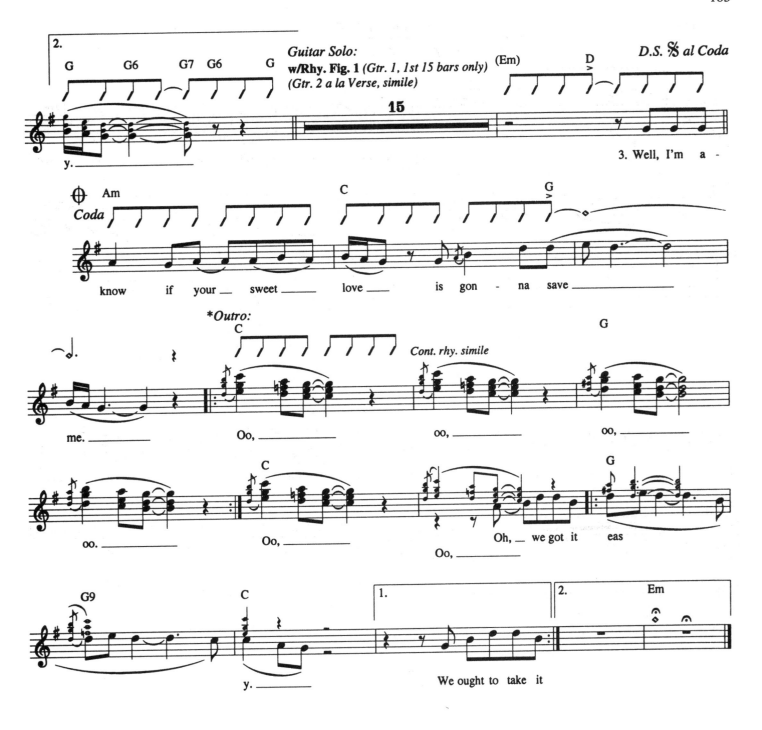

Verse 2:
Well, I'm a-standing on a corner in Winslow, Arizona,
And such a fine sight to see.
It's a girl, my lord, in a flatbed Ford
Slowing down to take a look at me.
(To Guitar Solo:)

Verse 3:
Well I'm a-running down the road,
Trying to loosen my load,
Gotta a world of trouble on my mind.
Looking for a lover who won't blow my cover,
She's so hard to find.
(To Chorus:)

Chorus 2:
Come on baby, don't say maybe.
I gotta know if your sweet love is gonna save me.
We may lose, and we may win.
Though we will never be here again.
So open up, I'm climbing in,
So take it easy.
(To Guitar Solo:)

Chorus 3:
Take it easy, take it easy.
Don't let the sound of your own wheels make you crazy.
Come on baby, don't say maybe.
I gotta know if your sweet love is gonna save me.
(To Coda)

Take It Easy - 4 - 4

TRUCKIN'

Words by
ROBERT HUNTER

Music by
JERRY GARCIA, BOB WEIR
and PHIL LESH

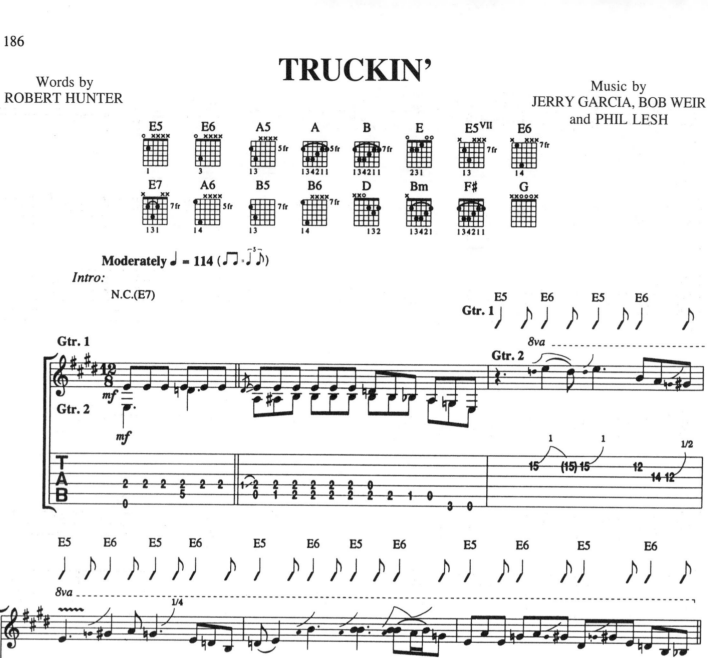

Chorus:

Truck - in', __ got __ my chips cashed __ in, __ keep __ truck - in', __ like the

Truckin' - 6 - 1

190

Chorus 5 :

Verse 2:
Most of the cats that you meet on street speak of true love.
Most of the time they're sitting and crying at home.
One of these days they know they gotta get going
Out of the door and down to the street all alone.

Chorus 2:
Truckin' like the doo da man.
Once told me you got to play your hand.
Sometimes the cards ain't worth a dime
If you don't lay them down.
(To Bridge:)

Verse 3:
What in the world ever became of sweet Jane?
She lost her sparkle, you know, she isn't the same.
Living on reds, vitamin C and cocaine,
All a friend can say is ain't it a shame.

Chorus 3:
Truckin' up to Buffalo. Been thinkin' you got to mellow slow.
It takes time, you pick a place to go,
And just keep truckin' on.

Verse 4:
Sitting and staring out of the hotel window.
Got a tip they're gonna kick the door in again.
I'd like to get some sleep before I travel,
But if you've got a warrant, I guess you're gonna come in.

Chorus 4:
Busted down on Bourbon Street,
Set up like a bowling pin,
Knocked down, it gets to wearing thin,
They just won't let you be.

Verse 5:
You're sick of hangin' around and you'd like to travel.
Get tired of traveling, you want to settle down.
I guess they can't revoke your soul for trying.
Get out of the door, light out and look all around.
(To Bridge:)

VINCENT
(Starry, Starry Night)

Words and Music by
DON McLEAN

Vincent (Starry, Starry Night) - 5 - 1

Vincent (Starry, Starry Night) - 5 - 2

194

Vincent (Starry, Starry Night) - 5 - 4

196

Vincent (Starry, Starry Night) - 5 - 5

WHITE ROOM

Words and Music by
JOHN BRUCE and
PETER CONSTANTINE BROWN

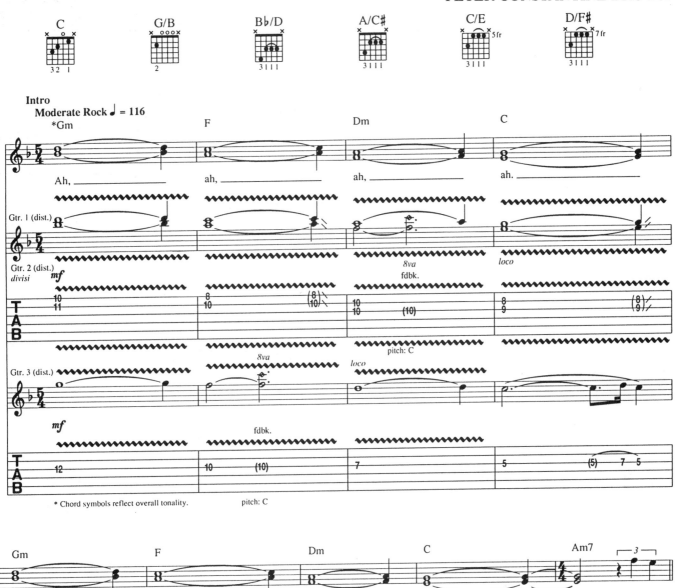

Intro
Moderate Rock ♩ = 116

* Chord symbols reflect overall tonality.

pitch: C

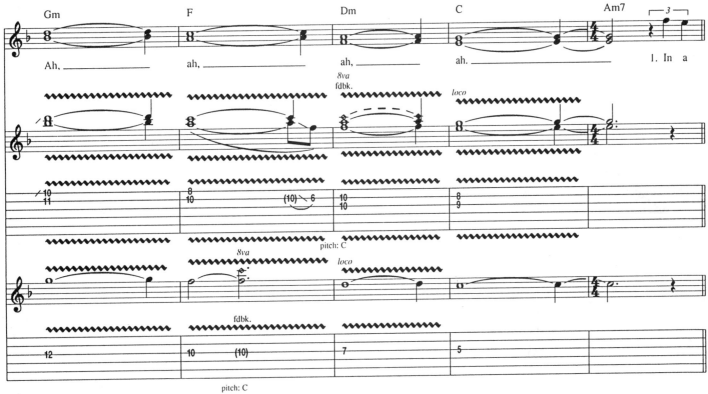

pitch: C

White Room - 11 - 1

Verse

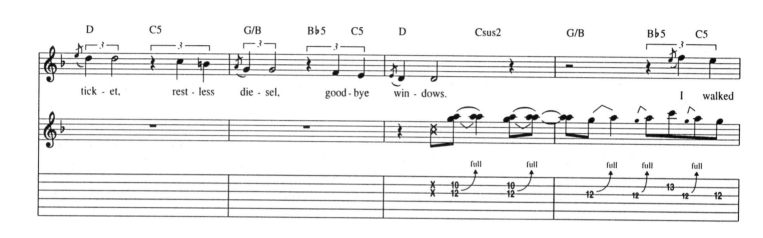

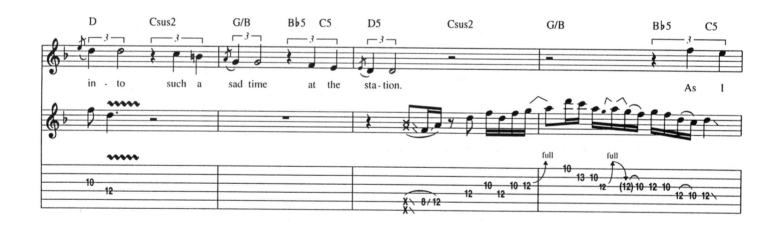

Bridge

Gtrs. 1 & 2: w/ Rhy. Figs. 2 & 2A

Gtr. 2: w/ Rhy. Fill 1

C — G/B — Bb/D — A/C#

wait ___ in the queue when the trains ___ come ___ back.

Gtr. 2: w/ Rhy. Fill 2

C — G/B — Bb/D — C/E — D/F#

Lie ___ with ___ you where the shad - ows run ___ from them - selves. ___

Interlude

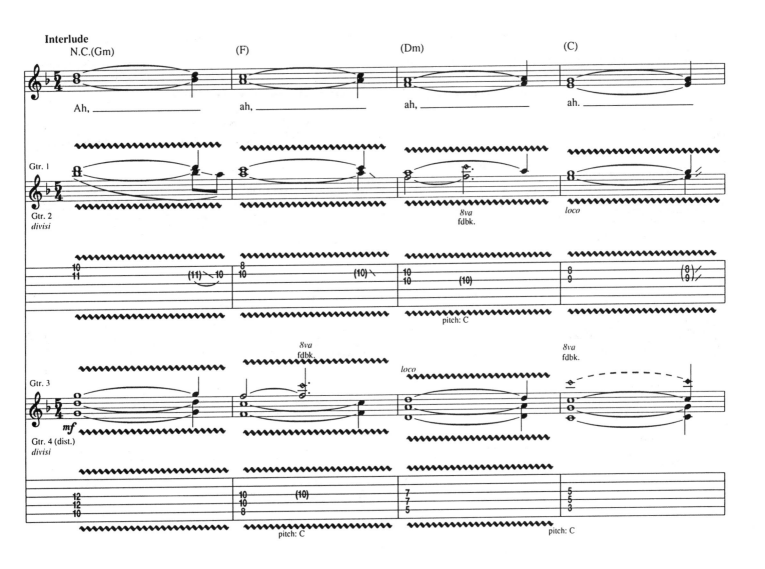

N.C.(Gm)   (F)   (Dm)   (C)

Ah, ___ ah, ___ ah, ___ ah.

Gtr. 1

Gtr. 2 divisi

8va fdbk.   loco

pitch: C

8va fdbk.   loco   8va fdbk.

Gtr. 3

mf

Gtr. 4 (dist.) divisi

pitch: C   pitch: C

Rhy. Fill 1
Gtr. 2

Rhy. Fill 2
Gtr. 2

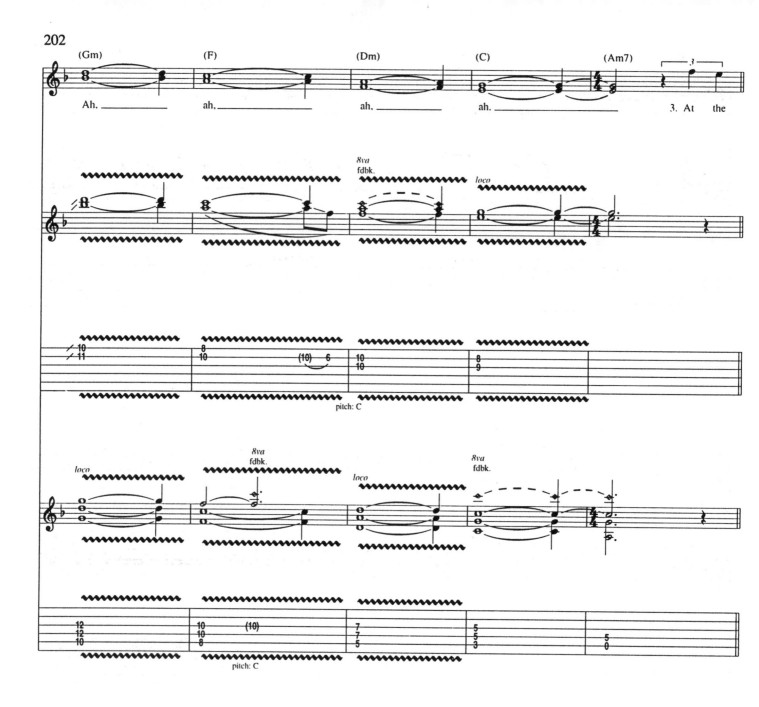

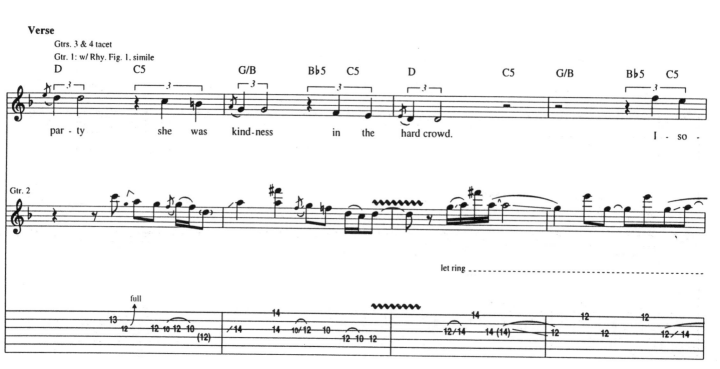

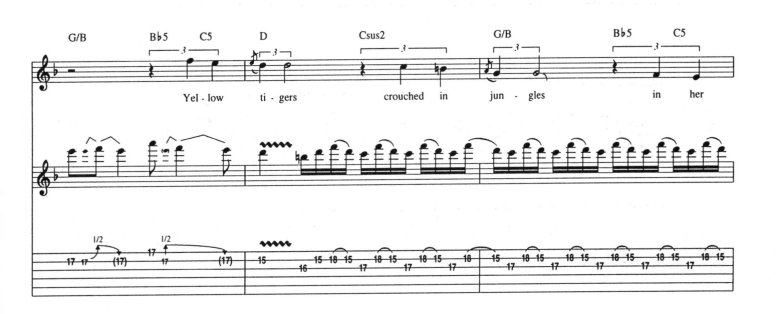

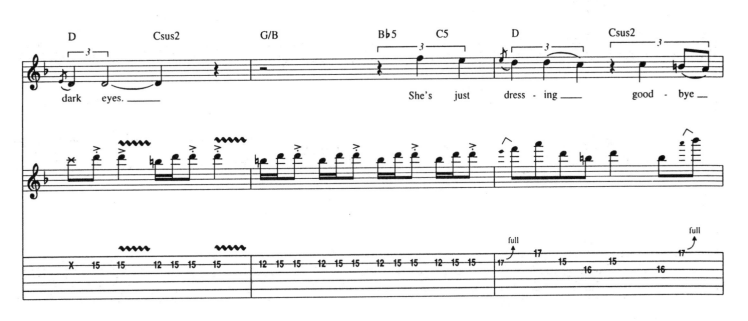

White Room - 11 - 7

204

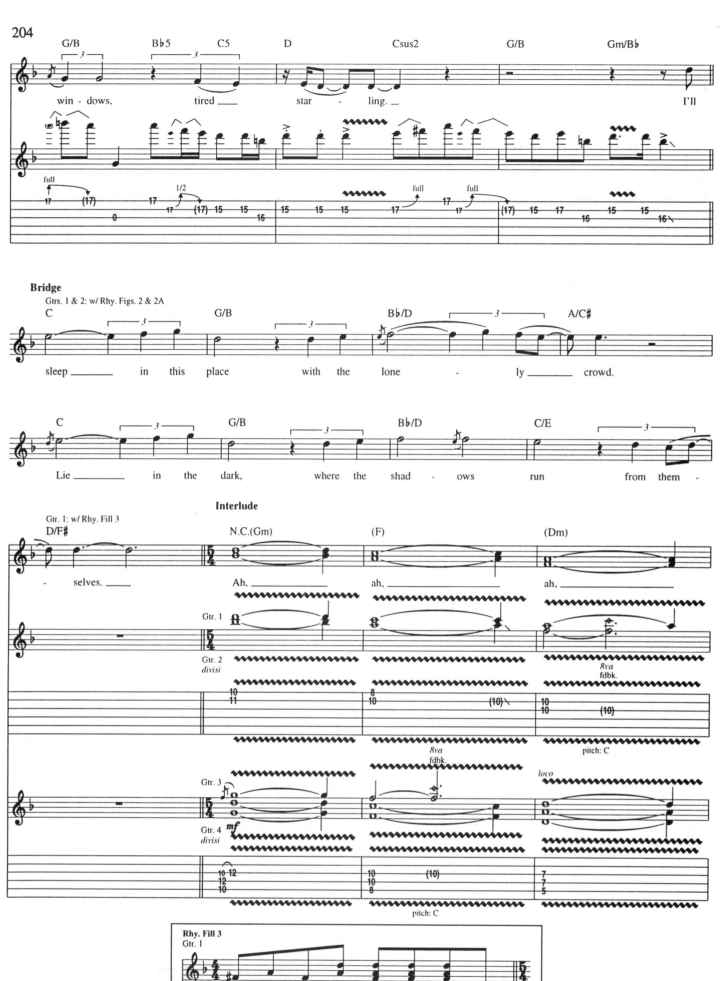

White Room - 11 - 8

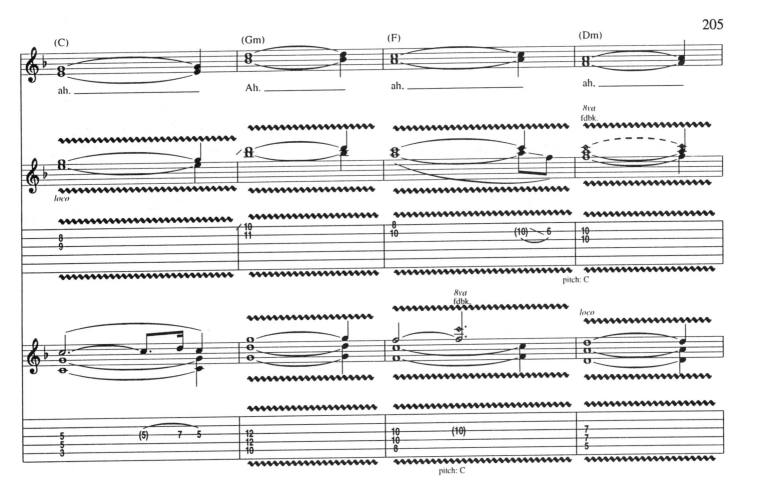

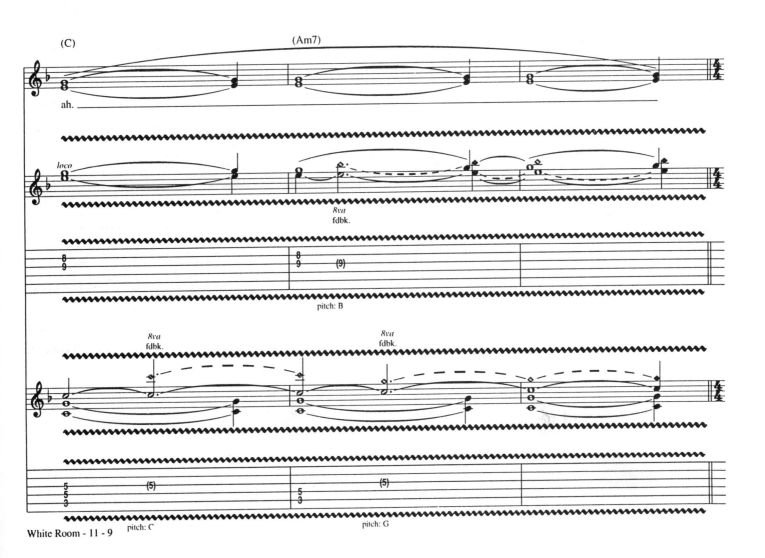

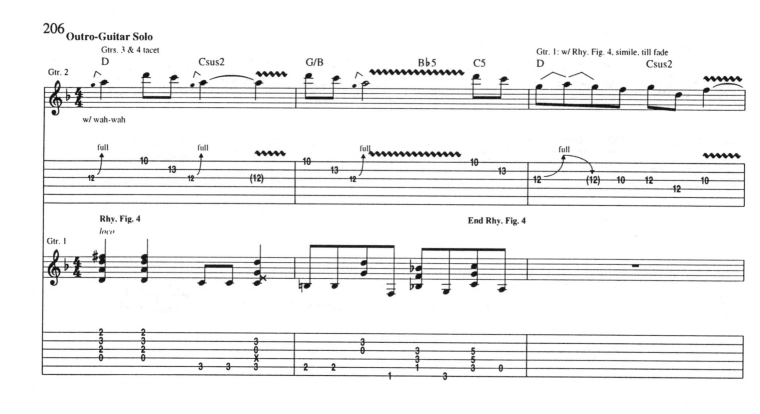

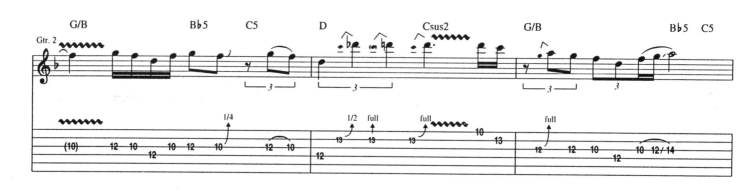

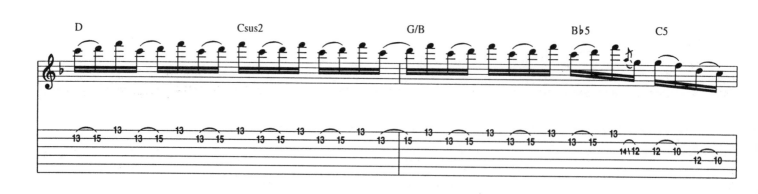

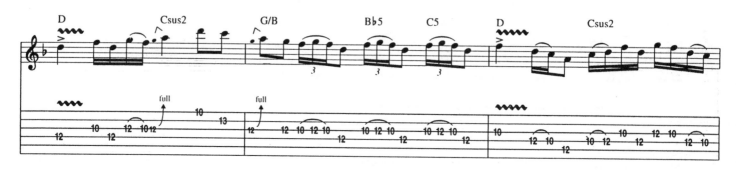

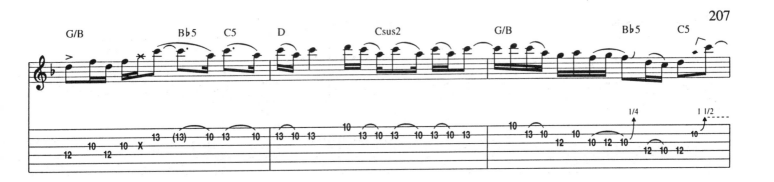

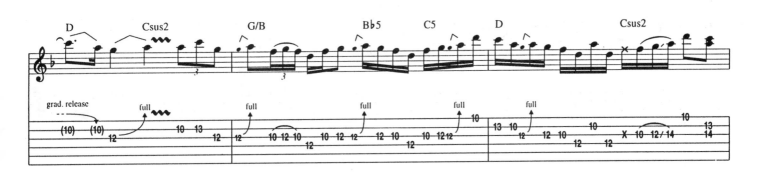

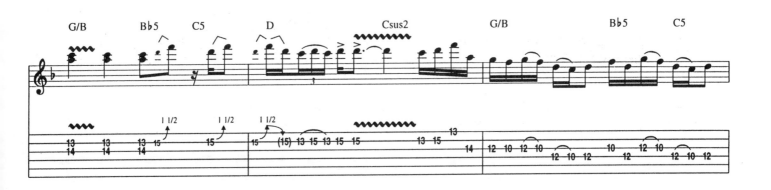

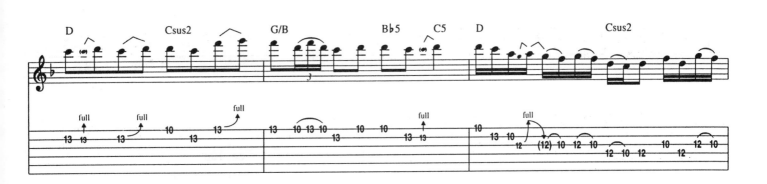

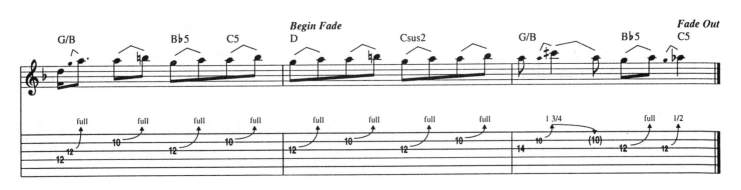

White Room - 11 - 11

WOODSTOCK

Words and Music by
JONI MITCHELL

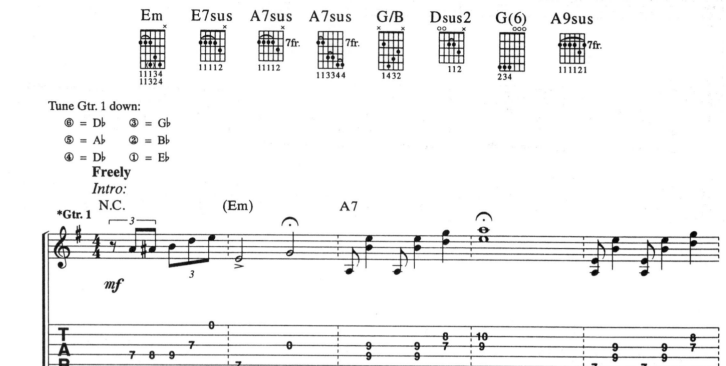

Tune Gtr. 1 down:
⑥ = D♭   ③ = G♭
⑤ = A♭   ② = B♭
④ = D♭   ① = E♭

Freely
Intro:

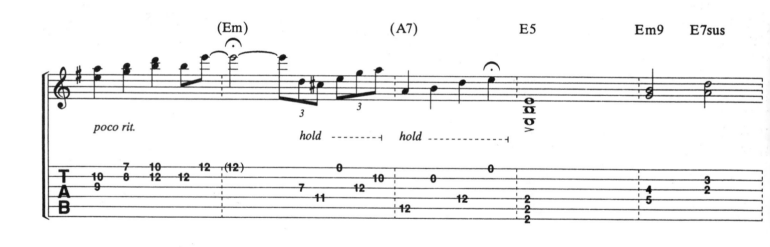

*Electric piano arranged for gtr.

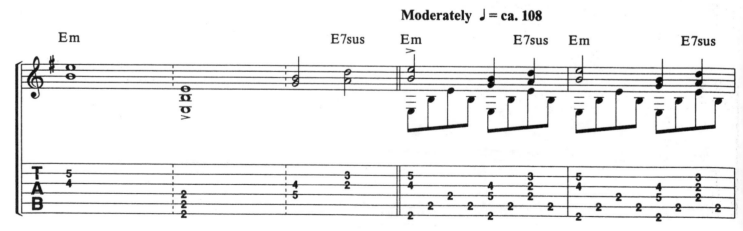

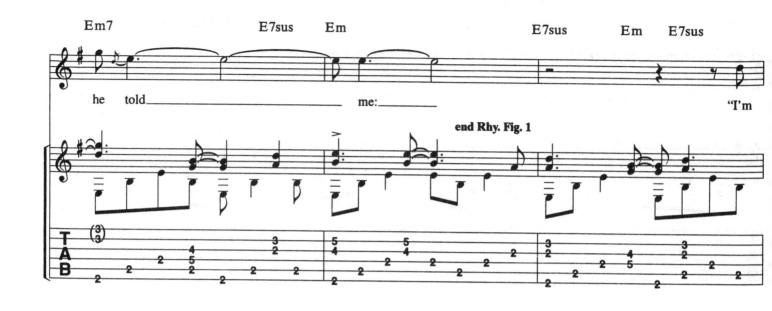

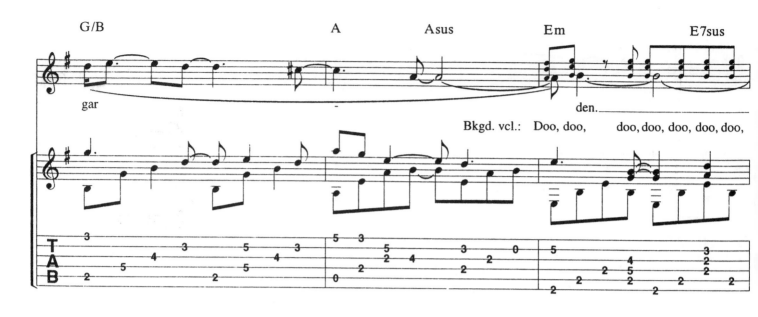

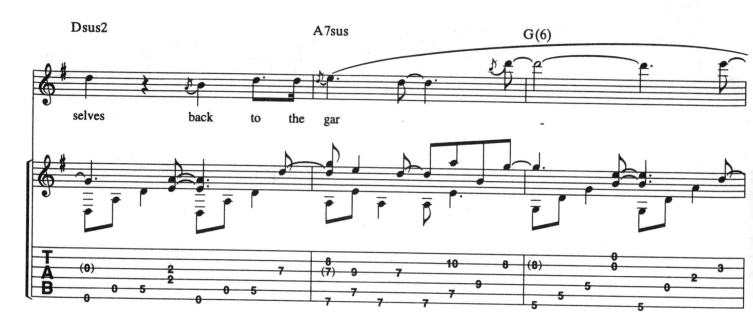

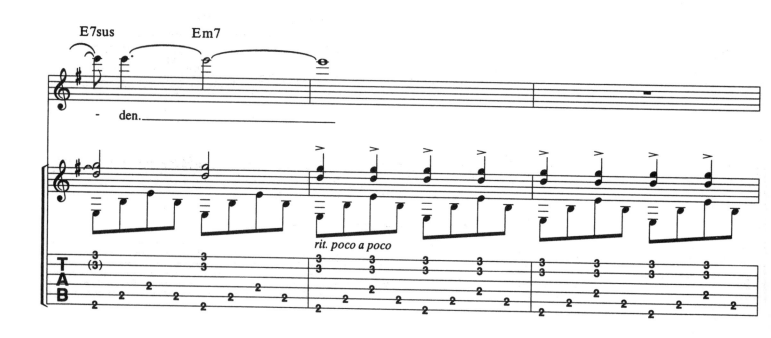

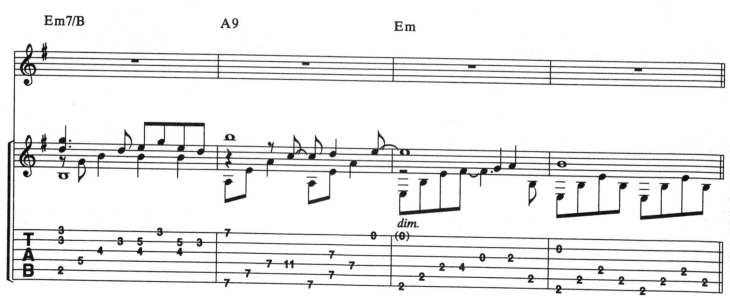

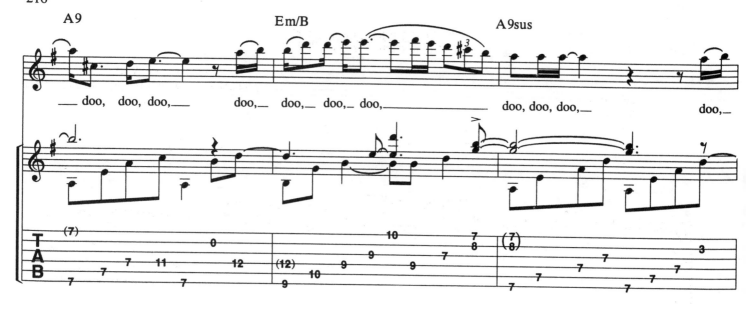

*Left-hand tap.
**Right-hand tap.

Verse 2:
Then can I walk beside you?
I have come here to lose the smog.
And I feel to be a cog
In something turning.
Well, maybe it is just the time of year,
Or maybe it's the time of man.
I don't know who I am,
But, you know, life is for learning.
(To Chorus:)

Verse 3:
By the time we got to Woodstock,
We were half a million strong,
And everywhere was song and celebration.
And I dreamed I saw the bombers
Riding shotgun in the sky,
And they were turning into butterflies
Above our nation.

YOUR SONG

Words and Music by
ELTON JOHN and BERNIE TAUPIN

*To match key of recording, tune down a 1/2 step.

Your Song - 3 - 1

Chorus:

I hope you don't mind,   I hope you don't mind _____   that I put down in

words _____   how _____ won - der - ful life _ is _ while you're _ in _ the world. _

Cont. in notation

Outro:

Verse 3:
I sat on the roof and kicked off the moss.
Well, a few of the verses, well, they've got me quite cross.
But the sun's been quite kind while I wrote this song.
It's for people like you that keep it turned on.

Verse 4:
So excuse me forgetting, but these things I do,
You see, I've forgotten if they're green or they're blue.
Anyway, the thing is, what I really mean . . .
Yours are the sweetest eyes I've ever seen.
(To Pre-chorus:)

YOU WEAR IT WELL

Words and Music by
ROD STEWART and MARTIN QUITTENTON

*Play on repeat only.

You Wear It Well - 8 - 2

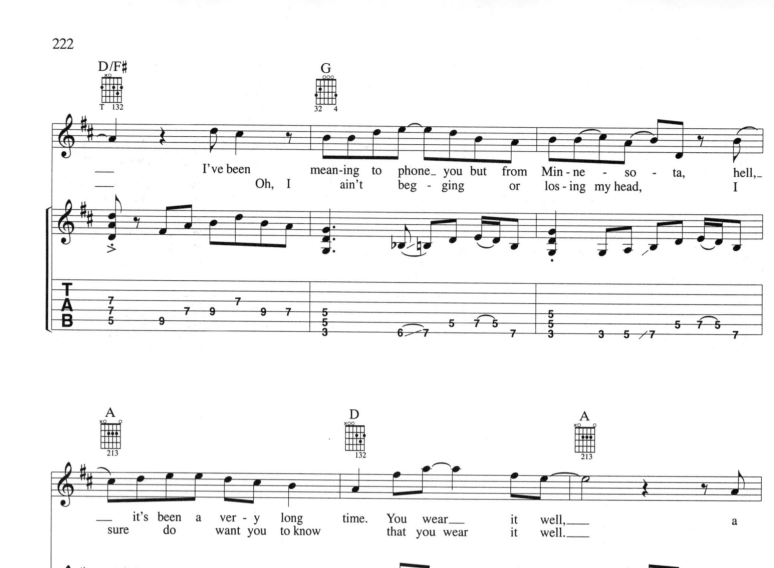

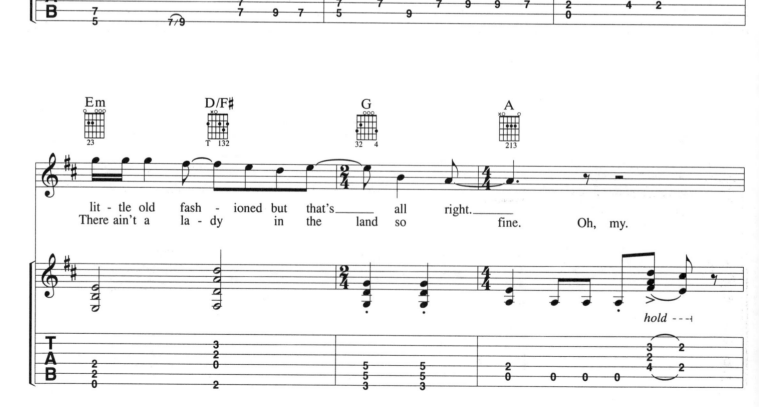

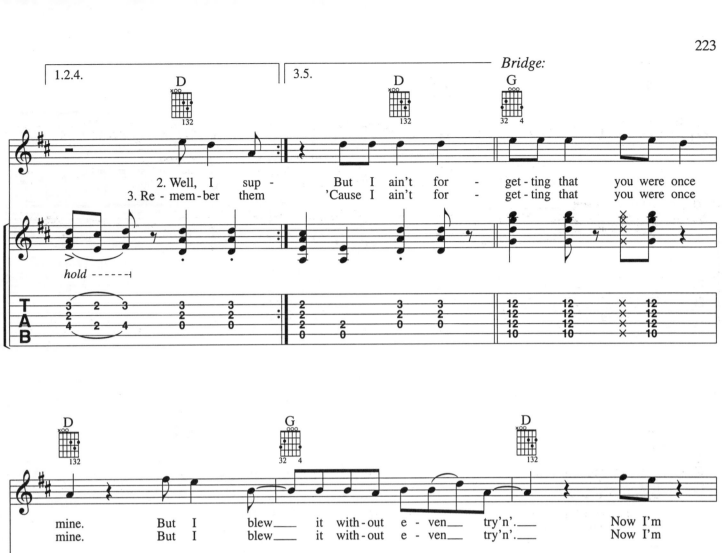

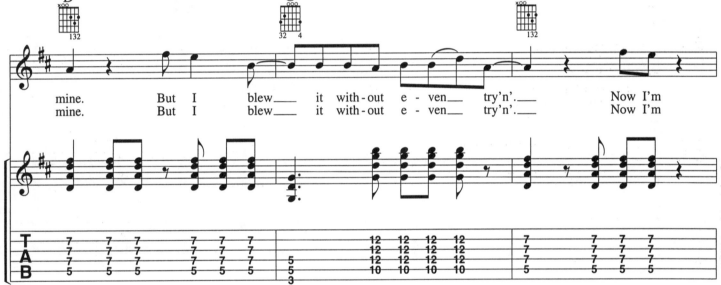

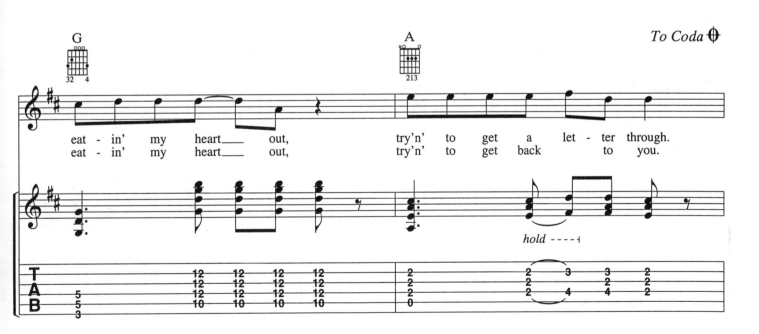

You Wear It Well - 8 - 4

Fiddle Solo:

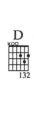

Composite arrangement.

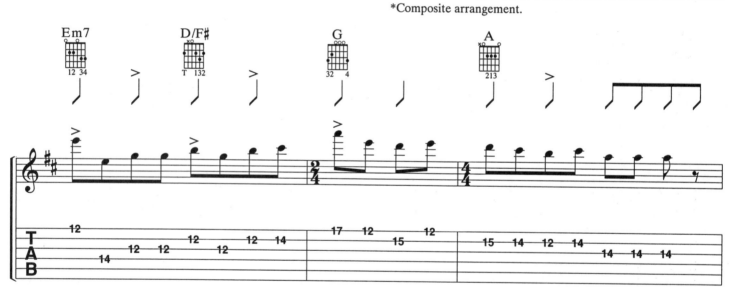

Cont. rhy. simile

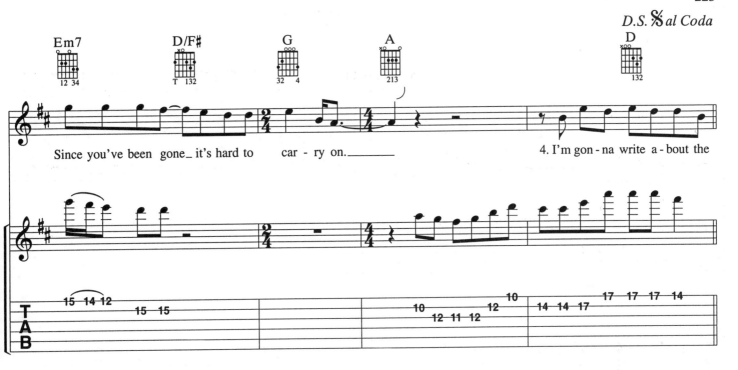

w/Rhy. Fig. 1 *(Acous. Gtr. 1) simile*

Af-ter all the years hope it's the same_ ad - dress._

end Rhy. Fig. 1

I love___ ya, I love___ ya, I love___ ya, ___ I love___ ya.

Repeat till fade

Oh, yeah.

Verse 3:
Remember them basement parties, your brother's karate.
The all day rock and roll shows.
Them homesick blues and radical views
Haven't left a mark on you.
You wear it well,
A little out of time but I don't mind.
(To Bridge:)

Verse 4:
I'm gonna write about the birthday gown that I bought in town.
When you sat down and cried on the stairs.
You knew it did not cost the earth, but for what it's worth,
You made me feel a millionaire.
And you wear it well,
Madame Onassis got nothing on you.

Verse 5:
Anyway, my coffee's cold and I'm getting told
That I gotta get back to work.
So when the sun goes low and you're home all alone,
Think of me and try not to laugh.
And I wear it well,
I don't object if you call collect.
(To Bridge:)

GUITAR TAB GLOSSARY **

TABLATURE EXPLANATION

READING TABLATURE: Tablature illustrates the six strings of the guitar. Notes and chords are indicated by the placement of fret numbers on a given string(s).

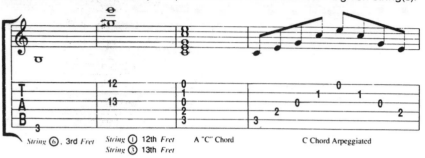

String ⑥, 3rd *Fret*   String ① 12th *Fret*   A "C" Chord   C Chord Arpeggiated
String ③ 13th *Fret*

BENDING NOTES

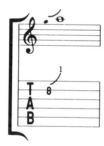

HALF STEP: Play the note and bend string one half step.*

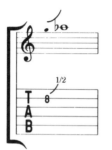

WHOLE STEP: Play the note and bend string one whole step.

PREBEND AND RELEASE: Bend the string, play it, then release to the original note.

RHYTHM SLASHES

STRUM INDICATIONS: Strum with indicated rhythm. The chord voicings are found on the first page of the transcription underneath the song title.

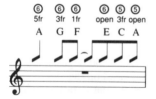

INDICATING SINGLE NOTES USING RHYTHM SLASHES: Very often single notes are incorporated into a rhythm part. The note name is indicated above the rhythm slash with a fret number and a string indication.

*A half step is the smallest interval in Western music; it is equal to one fret. A whole step equals two frets.

**By Kenn Chipkin and Aaron Stang

ARTICULATIONS

HAMMER ON: Play lower note, then "hammer on" to higher note with another finger. Only the first note is attacked.

PULL OFF: Play higher note, then "pull off" to lower note with another finger. Only the first note is attacked.

LEGATO SLIDE: Play note and slide to the following note. (Only first note is attacked).

PALM MUTE: The note or notes are muted by the palm of the pick hand by lightly touching the string(s) near the bridge.

ACCENT: Notes or chords are to be played with added emphasis.

DOWN STROKES AND UPSTROKES: Notes or chords are to be played with either a downstroke (⊓) or upstroke (∨) of the pick.